PAUL GAYLER'S
SAUCE book

PAUL GAYLER'S
SAUCE book

300 world sauces made simple · Photography by Richard Jung

Kyle Books

3 0645 11367885

This edition published in 2008 by Kyle Books, and imprint of Kyle Cathie Limited. general.enquiries@kyle-cathie.com www.kylecathie.com

Distributed by National Book Network 4501 Forbes Blvd., Suite 200, Lanham, MD 20706 Phone: (301) 459 3366 Fax: (301) 429 5746

ISBN 978-1-904920-84-7

Edited by Caroline Taggart
Designed by Jane Humphrey
Home economy by Linda Tubby
Styling by Roisin Nield
Copy editor Sally Somers
Proofreader Ruth Baldwin
Index by Sarah Ereira
Americanizer Delora Jones
Production director Sha Huxtable

Library of Congress Control Number: 2008939284

Printed in China by C&C Offset Printing Co.

Acknowledgements

I gratefully acknowledge the tremendous support of the following people, without whom this book would not have been possible:

Good friends Linda Tubby and Richard Jung, food stylist and photographer, who between them brought the sauces and recipes to life.

Roisin Nield, for her wonderful prop styling, as usual.

Jane Humphrey, for the gorgeous design.

Copy editor Sally Somers, for her support and putting the book together beautifully.

Jane Middleton, respected friend, for her help and advice.

Lara Mand, as ever, for a great job on the initial typing of the text.

My chefs, whose help on a daily basis and dedication to fine food help to make writing a book possible.

A special thanks to Caroline Taggart—I deeply value her support, friendship and professionalism in helping me create a lovely book.

DEDICATION
To my family, for their constant support for my writing,
and their encouragement.

contents

INTRODUCTION

A good sauce can make a meal. Think of a rich, creamy cheese béchamel poured over tender cauliflower florets, a sweet, aromatic tomato and basil sauce tossed with fresh pasta, or a light, vanilla-scented custard drizzled around a slice of apple pie—simple marriages made in heaven.

Sauce is a French word, originally taken from the Latin *salsus*, meaning salted. Classically, a sauce is a flavorful liquid that has been thickened in one of several standard ways and is used to accompany or coat a food. Nowadays, the definition has expanded to include not just classic French-style sauces but salsas, relishes, chutneys, and dressings, too. All these add flavor, color, texture, and moisture to food, and can even make it easier to digest.

For many, the idea of making at home the kind of sauces we enjoy in restaurants can be downright scary. But it's a lot easier than you might think, and doesn't have to be time-consuming or complex. Once you understand the various sauce "families" and have mastered a few basic techniques, it will open up the way to making a multitude of different sauces, and even creating your own versions. The key to success with sauces is to ensure that they complement and enhance the food they are to be served with. They should never overpower a dish, but should have a clean, well-defined flavor and a pleasing texture and consistency.

Although sauces are strongly associated with French cooking, they are an essential element in every cuisine. Now that global travel is available to all, we are more curious about the food of other cultures; at the same time our supermarkets stock a massive range of ingredients from all over the world. As a result, the scope for experimenting with sauces has increased enormously.

It's a shame that so many home cooks reach for a store-bought sauce rather than making their own. Commercial sauces are often laden with thickeners, colorings, preservatives, and other additives. They tend to have an unappetizing, gloopy consistency and frequently lack any flavor at all. Making fresh sauces at home will enhance your cooking beyond recognition. And although some require a degree of skill and judgement, others can be as simple as whizzing a few ingredients in a blender to make a pesto or relish, or briefly cooking berries with a little sugar to strain and serve as a fruit coulis.

When I set out to write this book, I wanted to show that creating great sauces was within the reach of any home cook. Many sauces can easily be put together in the time it takes for the rest of the meal to cook, and a surprising number of them require no cooking at all. Some, especially the French classics, take a bit longer and may need a good homemade stock to start with. If you don't have the time or the inclination to make your own stock, simply buy the best ready-made stock you can (the fresh ones in cartons are usually good, but check the ingredients: there shouldn't be anything in there you wouldn't use at home).

The book is divided into five geographical regions: France (covering the "classic" French sauces), Europe and the Mediterranean, the Americas, Asia, and the Pacific Rim. There is also a chapter on fusion food, called East Meets West, and one on sweet sauces. These divisions are not intended to be rigid, and there is plenty of overlap between the regions, so please don't feel constrained by them.

Sauces make a fantastic shortcut to different cultures and cuisines. You can give a piece of plain grilled fish or meat a French, Italian, Indian, or Mexican character, depending on whether you serve it with hollandaise, salmoriglio, raita, or chimichurri. You can flavor a basic sauce with hot chiles for an Asian or South American accent, with cheese, horseradish, or anchovies for a European feel, or with herbs and aromatics such as lemon and garlic for a taste of the Mediterranean. And when it comes to desserts: who can resist butterscotch sauce or a dark, rich hot chocolate sauce drizzled over ice cream?

A BRIEF HISTORY OF SAUCE-MAKING

In the days before refrigeration, sauces were often used to mask foods that were thought to be tainted in flavor. The Romans were the first to disguise dubious freshness in this way; they also used saucing as an opportunity to demonstrate the variety of costly spices the host had available. This practice continued well into the Middle Ages. Looking through old recipes in my own collection of cookbooks, I notice that sauces were often so heavily spiced and seasoned that it must have been almost impossible to single out any particular flavor, never mind taste the food underneath.

It was the French who developed the kind of sauces we are familiar with in the West today. At the beginning of the 19th century, Antonin Carême devised the first classification of sauces, based on five standard preparations, which he christened "mother sauces." These are espagnole (a brown, stock-based sauce thickened with flour and butter), demi-glace (a mixture of espagnole and brown stock that is reduced and usually nowadays thickened by simmering), béchamel (a milk-based white sauce thickened with flour and butter), velouté (a white sauce made with stock rather than milk), and tomato sauce. These five form the base from which all French sauces are derived. They are rarely served in their basic form; instead various ingredients and flavorings are added to make a particular sauce, transforming the original in minutes. The variations are known as "daughter sauces," for obvious reasons. Over time, the classic French repertoire was expanded by the addition of other sauces introduced from abroad. There is also a separate, smaller category of cold sauces, which are mostly derived from mayonnaise or vinaigrette.

By far the majority of classic sauces are thickened with starch, usually flour. However, during the nouvelle cuisine era of the 1970s, a small group of prominent chefs decided to eliminate starch as far as possible, in order to produce lighter sauces. The heavy, flour-thickened brown sauces were replaced by ones thickened with arrowroot or simply by boiling so that they reduced and thickened naturally. Butter sauces such as beurre blanc were suddenly fashionable, while veloutés became much lighter. This revolutionized sauce-making, and the more time-consuming sauces have never really come back into fashion. For the home cook, this is definitely good news.

So, too, is the revolution brought about by modern equipment. Blenders and food processors enable anyone to achieve a smooth, shiny, perfectly blended sauce. They have also coincided with the fashion for simple, colorful vegetable and herb purees that can be whizzed up in minutes and served as attractive and wholesome accompaniments to fish and meat.

French culinary traditions die hard, but today sauce-making is a much less structured affair than it used to be. Chefs can pick and choose from a variety of culinary traditions, and it is common to see a juxtaposition of styles and influences on restaurant menus. This in turn influences what we choose to eat at home, and sauce-making for the domestic cook has never been simpler or more accessible.

Author's note Each sauce recipe specifies how much it makes rather than how many people it serves. There is no set portion size with sauces —some people prefer a little; others, like me, enjoy plenty! So do use your own judgement to decide how much you need. All herbs used are fresh unless otherwise stated.

THE BASICS: GETTING STARTED

To make any good sauce, it is vital that you have a good base. This generally entails, in the case of sauce-making, a well-flavored stock. Stocks are the true foundation of sauces, especially in French cuisine. They are not in themselves difficult to make, but it can be a time-consuming process.

Unfortunately, there are no real shortcuts if you want a really good stock. The supermarket-made varieties sold in cartons are often weak in color and flavor, and bouillon cubes are worse still.

I have talked to many home cooks and it is fair to say very few of them make their own stocks. They express difficulty in finding bones, especially veal, game, and fish bones; normally chicken bones are the only available option. I urge you to find these more elusive bones by making friends with the people at your meat and fish counters, who will get them for you. Failing that, just use chicken bones: you will still achieve far better results than with cubes or store-bought stock.

Here are the basic stocks used throughout the book, which will help you get started on the road to producing great sauces. I find it best not to salt stock, as you might not know what sort of dish it will be used for later, and it is obviously much easier to add salt than take it away.

WHITE CHICKEN STOCK

A light chicken- or veal-based stock for soups and light sauces.

makes about 2 quarts

4½ pounds chicken carcass or bones (or a mixture of wings, legs, and carcass)

3 onions, cut into large chunks

2 large carrots, cut into large chunks

2 stalks of celery, cut into large chunks

2 leeks, white part only, chopped

4 sprigs of flat-leaf parsley

4 sprigs of thyme

1 Remove and discard any skin or obvious excess fat from the chicken. Place the chicken in a large pot, cover with cold water, and bring to a boil.

2 Drain the chicken and rinse out the pot. Put the chicken back in the pot and add 3 quarts water, to cover.

3 Bring to a boil, then simmer very gently, uncovered, for 1½ hours, skimming off any impurities that form on the surface of the stock from time to time. Add the vegetables and herbs and simmer for another hour.

4 Strain the stock into a large bowl and let it cool. It will keep for up to 1 week in the fridge or up to 6 months in the freezer.

WHITE VEAL STOCK

Instead of the chicken, use 4½ pounds of veal bones or trimmings, then proceed as for white chicken stock.

DARK CHICKEN, VEAL, OR BEEF STOCK

Roasting the meat trimmings and vegetables in the oven gives the stock a darker appearance and a richer, caramelized flavor. Suitable for dark jus-based sauces.

makes about 2 quarts

4½ pounds chicken, beef, or veal trimmings, cut into large pieces

2 tablespoons vegetable oil

3 onions, cut into large chunks

2 large carrots, cut into large chunks

4 stalks of celery, cut into large chunks

2 leeks, white part only, chopped

4 sprigs of flat-leaf parsley

4 garlic cloves

4 sprigs of thyme

2 tablespoons tomato paste

1 Preheat the oven to 400°F. Remove the skin or excess fat from the chicken, beef, or veal.

2 Heat the oil in a large flameproof roasting pan or ovenproof dish. Add the meat pieces and toss them in the hot oil.

3 Place in the oven and roast for 20–30 minutes, until golden all over.

4 Add the vegetables and herbs to the pan, mix them with the browned meat, and roast for another 30 minutes. Stir in the tomato paste and roast for a final 15 minutes.

5 Transfer to a large pot, cover with 3 quarts water and bring to a boil on the stove. Skim off any impurities that rise to the surface and simmer very gently, uncovered, for 3 hours.

6 Strain and cool, ready for use. This stock will keep for up to 1 week in the fridge or up to 6 months in the freezer.

FISH STOCK

makes about 2 quarts

1 tablespoon olive oil

2 onions, peeled and sliced

1 head of fennel, sliced

2 stalks of celery, sliced

2¼ pounds fish bones (preferably from white fish), chopped

⅔ cup dry white wine

1 sprig of thyme

1 small bay leaf

2 sprigs of tarragon

1 Heat the oil in a large pot and add the onions, fennel, and celery. Cook over a low heat until the vegetables have softened, about 10 minutes.

2 Rinse the fish bones in several changes of water to remove any blood traces, then add them to the pot. Cover and steam for 10 minutes.

3 Add the wine and simmer for 10 minutes.

4 Add the herbs and 2 quarts water to cover. Bring to a gentle simmer and cook, uncovered, for 20 minutes. Strain and cool. Fish stock will keep for up to 2 days in the fridge or 1 month in the freezer.

DASHI (ASIAN FISH STOCK)

This is a healthy, fragrant, and flavorsome stock, traditionally made from kombu, a brown seaweed native to Japan. You should be able to find both dried Kombu (sometimes labeled kelp) and bonito flakes in Oriental stores.

makes about 1 quart

⅔ ounce dried kombu

⅔ ounce dried bonito (tuna) flakes

1 Put the kelp into a pan with 4 cups cold water and let soak for 3 hours.

2 Bring to a boil and immediately remove the pan from the heat. Add a scant ½ cup cold water, then the bonito flakes.

3 Let them infuse for 15 minutes, then strain through a cheesecloth-lined strainer into a bowl. Dashi will keep for up to 2 days in the fridge or 1 month in the freezer.

VEGETABLE STOCK

Vegetable stocks are wonderful for adding flavor to vegetarian sauces, soups, and other dishes. Don't be tempted to use any old vegetables: some work better than others, and clearing out the vegetable drawer of your fridge is not the way to make good stock.

makes about 1 quart

3 large carrots, cut in half lengthwise

1 medium celeriac (celery root), cut into large chunks

2 stalks of celery, cut into large chunks

2 leeks, white part only, chopped

3 onions, quartered

7 ounces white button mushrooms, cut in half

1 head of fennel, outer leaves removed,
   cut into large chunks

3 garlic cloves

4 sprigs of flat-leaf parsley

4 sprigs of thyme

1 Put all the ingredients into a large pot and cover with 8 cups water.

2 Bring to a boil, then simmer, uncovered, for 1 hour. Strain the stock and let cool. Vegetable stock will keep for up to 1 week in the fridge or 6 months in the freezer.

DARK VEGETABLE STOCK

For a darker vegetable stock used for making a vegetarian jus, fry all the vegetables and herbs in a little butter and oil with 4 crushed vine tomatoes, then proceed as for the basic vegetable stock.

VARIETIES OF SAUCE

In the overall scheme of successful sauce-making, I think it's vitally important first to come to terms with all the types or varieties of sauce—the sheer scope available to the cook. Sauces fall into two very basic categories, hot and cold, but these can be broken down further as follows:

Emulsified butter sauces Hot white butter sauces, such as beurre blanc or beurre nantais, are traditionally made by reducing wine or vinegar with shallots, then emulsifying or thickening it with butter. Other hot butter sauces include brown butter, drawn butter, and noisette butter.

Cold butter sauces are known as compound butters and can be sweet or savory. These butters are not emulsified, but simply mixed and flavored with various other ingredients. They are served cold, placed over hot foods to melt on to them.

Pounded purees and coulis The cooked or raw strained puree of fruits such as soft berries, or tomatoes and vegetables, are pushed through a fine mesh strainer, then served hot or cold with various dishes. These include pounded sauces made using a mortar and pestle, such as Italian pesto or Asian nam jim.

Emulsified egg-enriched sauces These are rich yet light preparations based on eggs that are either slightly cooked through warming, then thickened with butter (as in hollandaise), or whisked raw, then thickened with oil (as for mayonnaise).

Traditional sabayon sauces (also known by their Italian name of *zabaglione*), made with eggs, wine, and sugar, are another form of emulsion sauce, and are especially popular throughout Europe. Crème anglaise (vanilla custard) is also an emulsified sauce, made with egg, milk, and cream.

Starch-thickened sauces These sauces are thickened using a roux base (see under *Ways of Thickening Sauces*, below), or by using arrowroot or cornstarch. Roux-based sauces include béchamel and velouté. Brown jus sauces tend these days to be thickened with arrowroot (or by natural reduction), to keep them clearer in color and flavor.

Gravies A gravy is a sauce made from the meat juices left in the pan after roasting or frying. Excess fat is removed from the cooking pan and replaced with wine, stock, or even water, which is then simmered vigorously into the caramelized juices. This is known as "de-glazing." Sometimes a little flour is mixed with the fat to make a roux and thicken the gravy.

Vinaigrettes and dressings These can be served warm, but are generally used cold to dress salads. They are usually composed of an acid—such as vinegar or lemon—emulsified with an oil base, mustards, and various seasonings.

Dipping sauces and salsas A dipping sauce is a common condiment, used to add flavor to a food. Unlike other varieties of sauce, which are applied to the food, in this case the food is dipped into the sauce. Dips are traditionally associated with finger foods and are prepared throughout the world, although the most popular originate in Asian and Pacific Rim countries. These include various mayonnaises, guacamole, raita, ketchups, sour cream dips, Asian fish sauces, and barbecue sauces.

Salsas are traditionally associated with Spanish or Latin American cooking; *salsa* is the Spanish word for sauce, and has come to denote a degree of spiciness. They are almost always uncooked (with a few exceptions), and are roundly flavored with spices in the form of varying heats of chile and with other aromatic herbs and seasonings.

Ketchups and relishes These usually take the form of preserved sauces, which are, I feel, indispensable to the cook's repertoire. They are available ready-made, but are easy to make at home, can be prepared well in advance, and need no last-minute attention. Ketchup, condiment-style relishes such as horseradish, and long-cooked chutneys all fall into this category.

Also included are the Asian and Oriental sauces such as soy sauce (made from fermented soybeans) and Thai and Vietnamese fish sauces (from fermented salt-dried fish and shellfish). Chinese sauces include hoisin, oyster sauce, plum sauce, and numerous others. Many are used in cooking as well as for a dipping sauce and condiment.

Flavored syrup sauces Sweet preparations of sugar and water (or fruit juice), cooked until clear and often flavored with herbs or spices, are easy to make and extremely versatile for desserts.

WAYS OF THICKENING SAUCES

Sauces generally should not be watery in consistency; they can be thickened by one or a combination of the following:

Roux A roux is a mixture of equal parts of melted butter and flour. The two are combined in a pan and cooked to varying degrees, according to the type of roux needed, before the liquid is added. A white roux is cooked just lightly, without browning, as in the case of béchamel.

A blond mix is cooked slowly and for longer, until it is sandy in texture and has a pale biscuit color; it is used for velouté sauces.

Brown roux is cooked over a gentle heat for even longer, until the flour has turned brown but the butter has not burned. It is traditionally used for demi-glace (half-glaze) sauce (a rich brown sauce used in French cuisine either as a base for other sauces or on its own). However, it is relatively rare these days, even in professional kitchens, where lighter, thickened natural meat stocks, known as *jus lié*, are favored.

Cornstarch and arrowroot need to be "slaked," which means dissolved, in a little cold water or wine before being added to the hot liquid. They are then stirred in and the sauce thickens almost immediately. This method gives a more refined, clear sauce than thickening with a roux and is particularly popular in Chinese dishes and sweet sauces. As a general guideline, 1 teaspoon slaked cornstarch or arrowroot will thicken 7 ounces (a scant cup) sauce. I recommend cornstarch for thickening milk and dairy-based sauces and arrowroot for meat sauces, as this adds a superior glossy sheen to the sauce, as well as giving better "mouth feel."

Eggs and cream Egg yolks in particular are used as a thickening base of many of the emulsion sauces, such as hollandaise. Egg yolks combined with cream and added to sauces are known as "liaisons"; these are used to thicken and enrich classic velouté sauces, by being added in the last minute of cooking. Liaisons must be added quickly and while the sauce is away from the heat, before being returned to a low heat to thicken. As for custard, it must be stirred constantly until the point where it coats the back of a spoon. The sauce must not boil, or it will curdle, resulting in a scrambled-egg appearance. This thickening method is perhaps the most intimidating for the beginner, and may take a bit of practice. But since today's velouté sauces are made with a cream reduction, rather than with flour, the sauces tend to be rich enough so you don't need to add a liaison at the end.

Beurre manié (kneaded butter) is a paste-like mixture, made with a ratio of two parts butter to one part flour. It is sometimes also called an "uncooked roux," the difference being that the butter is not melted as it is for a roux. Beurre manié is added to the hot cooking liquid in small lumps, and whisked evenly for quick thickening.

Butter Chilled butter whisked in small pieces into a hot sauce, away from the heat, has a two-tier effect: it gives body and shine to the sauce and acts as a thickener. In the professional kitchen this is known as *monter au beurre*. It can be useful for correcting a sauce that has gone wrong or needs improving (see pages 23 and 30).

Vegetable, fruit, and nut purees Many cooked vegetables, fruits, and nuts may be pureed to great advantage for use in sauces. Often the resulting sauces can be lighter in texture, prettier in color, and generally more interesting. For example: shallots, mushrooms, and potatoes in the Greek potato sauce skordalia; tomatoes in a classic tomato sauce; herbs in an Italian pesto, and nuts for a peanut sauce. Pureeing vegetables and fruits gives a sauce body as well as a silken texture, without the addition of dairy products; it is therefore a useful low-fat and allergy-free option. Generally these sauces are processed in the blender to thicken them, then strained through a fine mesh strainer.

Natural reduction You will notice when making the sauces in this book that it often says "reduce by half." This is in fact the simplest technique for thickening a sauce and simply means reducing a thin liquid in quantity by evaporation; the result is a thickened sauce with a more intense flavor.

An uncovered pan over a fairly high heat is the usual way to reduce a sauce. To speed up the process, it can simply be transferred to a wider pan: the greater surface area means evaporation will be faster.

In general, this method is used only when making brown sauces, although some cream-based sauces can be prepared in a similar way. However, cream sauces have a tendency to scorch easily around the edges if they are not monitored regularly as they cook and reduce; the process also needs to be a slower, gentler one.

When reducing any sauce, it is vitally important not to season it, as the flavor will be intensifying as it reduces down, and the results might be too salty. Any impurities that form on the surface need to be skimmed off, to keep the sauce clear and shiny.

Other methods of thickening Bread is sometimes used to thicken a sauce, especially in the Mediterranean region, as in the Catalan romescu sauce, Turkish tarator, and Italian agliata, and not forgetting traditional bread sauce (see page 72), served with roasted birds in Britain for centuries.

There are some sauces, traditionally fowl- or game-based ones, that use animal blood as a thickening agent. This is known as a blood liaison, but it is rarely made these days because of restrictions placed on raw blood preparation.

TRICKS OF THE TRADE

In all professions, in addition to technical know-how, there is a handful of useful tricks of the trade, and cooking is no different. Here are some sauce-making tips that I have gained with the experience of many years: over time, they will help you to be more proficient.

THE RIGHT CONSISTENCY

Pouring consistency I always instruct my cooks that a sauce to be served poured over a piece of meat or fish, or as a coating for vegetables, should have a "pouring consistency." This simply means it should be thin enough to pour, but not so thin as to be watery. When ready, the sauce should coat the back of a serving spoon lightly, rather than run right off.

A simple test is to run your finger along the back of the sauce-dipped spoon: if the sauce runs slowly back together, it is ready. This was one of the first things I learned as a young chef, and I still use it as a guideline to this day.

Coating consistency A sauce that is to cling to the ingredients with which it is served calls for a "coating consistency"; in other words, a slightly thicker consistency than pouring. This could involve anything from saucing a pasta dish, to coating a vegetable with mornay sauce, or other gratin-style dishes. Sauces of this type tend to be based on béchamels or veloutés.

Thick consistency This should be thick enough to bind a mixture for fillings, stuffings, or soufflé bases. Again, these are generally béchamel- and velouté-based preparations.

BALANCING OR IMPROVING FLAVOR

A sauce lacking flavor For brown sauces: add a splash of port or Madeira—it will improve the flavor and color, providing sweetness and depth.

For white sauces (especially veloutés): add a splash of white wine or champagne to fish sauces, and a little port or Madeira to chicken-based veloutés.

Lacking piquancy or bite If a sauce tastes a little dull and flat, a touch of acidity—a squeeze of lemon juice or some wine vinegar—will lift it.

Lacking color Generally speaking, a sauce lacking in color means the bones used in the sauce (or for that matter in the base stock) have been inadequately caramelized during roasting. It is vitally important that they, and the vegetables, are cooked to a deep golden brown. Insufficient coloring produces a pale jus. The addition of a tablespoon of soy sauce can help to improve the color of a sauce.

Too fatty If a sauce appears too fatty, simply add an ice cube and bring it to a boil; you can then ladle off the fat and impurities that rise to the surface.

Too sharp a flavor The addition of a spoonful or two of cream, a little unsalted butter and some sugar, or better still red currant jelly, will take an overly sharp edge off a sauce.

Adjusting the seasoning You will see throughout the recipes in the book a note to adjust seasoning at the end of certain recipes. But how do you know what is the correct seasoning? What is too little? What is too much? This knowledge will usually come with experience, although there are a few things to consider in the meantime. Remember too that everyone has a different sense of taste, so what seems like perfection to you may seem bland to someone else.

As a rule, "adjust seasoning" simply refers to good old salt and pepper. If you like (and it has to be personal) the way a sauce tastes as it is, don't add anything. However, if you think it is missing something, you might need to add a little more of one of the ingredients. For example, sometimes a particular herb is used to accentuate a sauce: if it is not discernible, add a little more.

FINISHING TOUCHES

Below are some tips for balancing certain aspects of the finished sauce. They generally apply to brown sauces, with a few for velouté-based ones.

In professional kitchens, brown sauces are generally finished with small knobs of chilled butter just before serving (the technique called *monter au beurre*). This has a three-tiered effect on your sauce: it lightly thickens it, enriches it, and creates a smoother texture. Once the butter is added, the sauce should never be reboiled; it will come out of suspension and float on the surface, rendering your sauce somewhat greasy. Cream sauces are also sometimes finished with a little butter, but I find this unnecessary in terms of flavor. The only advantage is that it may add a little extra richness and shine if these are lacking. As well as last-minute addition of butter, sauces are often given a final touch of freshly chopped herbs, which help to finish and enhance the sauce.

Skimming sauces I think of skimming a sauce to keep it clear of foam, fat, and impurities as applying a touch of TLC, giving it loving care which will pay dividends to the final result. It is one of the most important, yet overlooked, steps in making fine sauces and soups—and, for that matter, jams. The skimming should take place during the cooking process, any impurities being carefully removed with a small ladle. This will ensure that your sauce does not become cloudy and dull in appearance, but remains clear and shiny. Make it a habit: you will find it improves the general quality of your cooking.

Allowing flavors to develop You will notice with certain sauces, namely salsa and the dipping sauces of Asia, that the recipe often calls for the sauce to be left on hold for a few hours after it is made, to allow flavors to meld together. This ensures that the flavors bloom, that acids calm down, and aromatics and spices intensify—so producing a more complex and flavorful sauce.

Fresh and dried herbs and spices I am often asked, can I use dried herbs when making sauces? I have to say that with the exception of dried rosemary, thyme, and bay leaves, I have little time for them; I always use fresh herbs in preference. Soft herbs—namely chives, tarragon, basil, and cilantro—should ideally be chopped at the last minute (or as near to the last minute as possible), then stirred into the finished sauce. A hardy style of herb—such as rosemary or thyme—can be cooked in the sauce.

When using spices, it is best to crush or grind them as they are needed, because they can quickly lose their impact in cooking. One good way to help ensure that you have aromatic herbs and spices is to always buy them in small amounts. Remembering to top them up little and often means you won't have unused quantities turning stale.

MAKING SAUCES AHEAD OF TIME

Although making sauces ahead of time undoubtedly offers a great advantage to any cook, there are certain factors to consider. How to keep a sauce hot, in safe conditions and ready for serving, is the main consideration. Reheating it, and storing it correctly for later use, are other important ones.

Keeping it hot and ready to serve When a sauce is ready, it needs to be kept hot until ready for serving. To do this, I suggest using a bain-marie (water bath) or double boiler. Because the heat is indirect, it is especially good for keeping emulsified sauces warm, such as hollandaise, béarnaise, or other butter-based sauces which are less stable than classic white and brown sauces. It is also ideal for keeping other sauces hot.

Place the still warm prepared sauce in the top of a double boiler or, for a stovetop water bath, place the bowl of prepared sauce in a large saucepan. Add enough hot water to the pan to come up the sides of the bowl and keep it below boiling point. Even if the water in the stovetop bain-marie boils, the contents of the sauce bowl will not.

To prevent skin from forming on the surface of your finished sauce, cover it with a piece of lightly buttered baking parchment prior to placing it in the bain-marie, or else use a piece of foil to seal the top of the bowl. I have also discovered over the years that all sauces, but especially emulsified sauces, can successfully be kept warm in a vacuum thermos (see Equipment, page 17).

Reheating a sauce Reheating does not mean recooking; it simply means bringing it back to the temperature of the pre-made sauce. For some sauces (cream sauces or white sauces) this needs to be done very slowly, as they tend to burn or scorch easily. Brown sauces, on the other hand, can be brought back to a boil over a high heat.

Storing a finished sauce A sauce you are intending to store should be allowed to cool completely, before being covered with plastic wrap, to prevent a skin from forming and to keep it free of any bacterial growth. It should then be put in the fridge, where it will stay fresh and unharmed.

A NOTE ON EQUIPMENT

Pans and frying pans In the French kitchen, copper pans were originally used in classic sauce-making. Nowadays these have been replaced by lighter stainless steel varieties, which are more commonly used even in the professional environment.

Select various sizes of pans and frying pans, ideally heavy-bottomed and well balanced, as they conduct the heat better. Large pans or stock pots are necessary for making stock in large quantities. Avoid buying cheap aluminum pans, which may react with ingredients such as the acid component of lemons or vinegar.

Nonstick pans have many uses and are especially good for dry-frying spices, so have at least one handy in the kitchen.

A wok is another useful piece of pan equipment, especially when preparing Asian dishes. Woks vary hugely in quality, but it's worth buying a good, sturdy, cast iron one with a heavy base. Like all cast iron pans, a wok should not be washed in the conventional way, with detergent, but should be wiped clean, and kept oiled between uses.

Strainers As with pans, it is handy to keep various sizes of strainers, with different degrees of fineness: some for achieving smooth purees and sauces, and others for clear sauces. The finer your strainer, obviously the more refined your finished sauce will be. In years past, tamis cloth was used to produce the ultimate smooth and glossy sauces, but for exceptionally fine straining this has all but disappeared and been replaced by fine cheesecloth.

Choose stainless steel strainers, which do not corrode with time.

Whisks A stainless steel balloon whisk with a large, firm handle is vital. A selection of sizes will allow you to use one appropriate to the size of your pan, but save the larger ones for whipping egg whites and cream, and choose a smaller one for sauces. Similarly, egg beaters are fine for beating egg whites or cream, but not for sauce-making.

Small coil whisks seem to be extremely popular these days, and are excellent for small jobs and for getting into the corners of pans while sauce-making. Apart from the practical advantages when making sauces, whisks help to add gloss and shine, especially to white sauces made with stock or milk.

Wooden spoons, and spatulas Wooden spoons are best for sauce-making and some other preparations, such as frying, as they do not conduct heat. As well as being cheap and easy to find, they are also the best for use with nonstick frying pans, which are easily scratched.

Spatulas, especially long, flexible ones, are ideal for getting the last bit of food out of pans, and for scraping bowls. A selection of various sizes is handy.

Ladles and skimmers Stainless steel ladles are very useful for transferring liquids from pan to food processor or strainer, and for pushing them through a fine strainer. Again, having a variety of sizes means you can match them to the job in hand.

Skimmers are like flat, perforated spoons and are generally used to remove fat or other impurities that float to the surface of stocks and sauces.

Blenders and food processors These days blenders can make light work of simple preparations such as pesto. They are also good for breaking down food before it is pushed through a fine mesh strainer to achieve a smoother-textured sauce. It is worth investing in a robust, heavy-duty blender, as it will last much longer than a cheaper version. Hand-held blenders are excellent for pureeing sauces in the pan—especially those in small quantities that would get lost in a regular blender—and they take up less storage space. Food processors do the job of the blender, plus much more. With their different blades, they can chop, mix, grate, and slice.

In some recipes where the quantities are very small, I advise using a small blender. You can now buy mini blenders to have alongside your larger-bowled blender, but another good option for small quantities of herb and spice mixtures is to use a small coffee grinder, kept especially for this purpose so that no coffee flavor is imparted.

Graters The easiest way to grate lemon, lime, or orange zest is with a fine microplane grater. Unlike with a box grater, the zest doesn't all stick to the grater, you don't grate your fingers, and you can produce fine flecks of zest that more or less dissolve into the sauce you are making. If you buy one with a medium as well as a fine zesting attachment, you will find them endlessly versatile in the kitchen.

Mortars and pestles Before blenders and food processors became the norm, much of the hard work of making pureed sauces was carried out with a mortar and pestle, a versatile duo also used for crushing spices and similar preparations. Many sauces, especially those from Asia, rely on this piece of equipment to make liquid-based sauces,

so if you don't already own a mortar and pestle, I would urge you to buy one. Choose a heavy, fairly large one, with a non-reactive surface. In Asia, they are traditionally made of stone or granite, which are much more effective than some glass and wood varieties on the market.

Mixing bowls Again, you want a good selection of stainless steel bowls, in various sizes. They are ideal for holding strained sauces and for making sauces and dressings. As well as different sizes, choose some that are shallow and some with high sides.

Roasting pans More often used for roasting the bones or vegetables for stock-making, a roasting pan can in fact act as an excellent bain-marie, or water bath—in the oven or, if it's flame-proof, on the stove—to keep a sauce in another container hot (see page 15).

Measuring cups These are essential for accurate volume measuring when following a recipe; stainless steel or toughened glass are the best. Plastic measuring cups have the practical advantage of being lighter and more manageable when full, but they tend to scratch easily, which can make the measurements hard to read.

Vacuum thermos You may be surprised to see a vacuum thermos as a piece of sauce-making equipment, but I find it useful for keeping all sorts of sauces either hot or cold, from a rich brown sauce to a delicate emulsion such as hollandaise or béarnaise. Purchase a well-made, sturdy thermos.

DAUBE   45
STOCKFISH   40
SOUPE AU PISTOU   45
PÂTES FRAÎCHES ou POLENTA   60
                                               35
NAPOLITAINE   35
BOLOGNAISE   35
PISTOU   35
DAUBE   35
GRATIN D'AUBERGINE   45
                                               45

— BOIS...
PE...

PÂTI...

Lou Picha Leva

Poivron farci + salade + frites   45

Lasagnes + salade   45

Calamars à la Niçoise .   45

Soupe au pistou   35

Ratatouille + salade + frites   40

Jambon + salade + frites   35

Poulet + salade + frites   45

Aïoli   (Vendredi)   35

Pâtes fraiches   45

Porchetta + salade frites .   45

FRENCH classics

It might seem daunting to start this book with the mind-blowing array of classic French sauces. This chapter is inevitably far more regimented than the ones that follow, but all the sauces are well within the grasp of anyone who is prepared to learn a few basics. With practice, you will soon feel confident enough to produce them for any occasion.

I have always believed that French cooking owes its fame largely to its wonderful repertoire of sauces. They represent the pinnacle of culinary technique and can transform virtually any dish into something elegant, refined, and delicious: think of glorious, golden hollandaise sauce, a smooth, light velouté (the name means "velvety" in French), or a concentrated, savory, slow-simmered brown sauce, based on a rich meat stock. I have also included many of my favorite variations on the classic themes—and would encourage you to experiment with other possibilities of your own.

EMULSIFIED SAUCES

Emulsified sauces are sauces that are thickened (or emulsified) with egg yolks and either warm butter (hot emulsions) or oil (cold emulsions).

Chief among these sauces are the famous mayonnaise, hollandaise, and white butter-based sauces such as beurre blanc. In simple terms, they are formed by an emulsion of fat droplets (butter or oil) combined with a liquid (vinegar, water, or stock) and occasionally stabilized with an egg yolk, as in the case of mayonnaise or hollandaise.

These sauces are rich, smooth, and luxuriously subtle, but are often thought to be the most intimidating of sauces for beginners to master. Following the instructions to the full, however, will bring success and confidence in time.

PG tip—clarifying butter Most classic recipes for hollandaise call for clarified butter. It is not essential, but the sauce will be creamier and smoother than if you use just melted butter. To clarify butter, gently melt it in a small pan. Skim the froth from the surface using a small ladle or spoon, then carefully tip the butter into a clean pan or sauceboat, leaving the milky sediment behind. Set aside until tepid and discard the sediment.

Unsalted butter is better for clarifying than salted butter. Clarified butter can be heated to higher temperatures than ordinary butter, making it also ideal for cooking processes such as sautéing.

HOLLANDAISE

Hollandaise sauce as we know it today is the modern descendant of an earlier sauce, believed to have been brought to France by the Huguenots. For me it is the finest of all the warm, emulsified butter sauces—delicious and subtle. ⊕ *It is wonderful served with poached fish, poached eggs, and vegetables. The quantities here are enough to sauce 8–10 servings.*

makes 1¾ cups

2 tablespoons white wine vinegar
2 tablespoons water
1 teaspoon lightly crushed white peppercorns
4 egg yolks from cage-free eggs
2¼ sticks unsalted butter, clarified (see tip below)
juice of ½ lemon
salt and freshly cracked black pepper
a pinch of cayenne pepper

1 Put the vinegar, water, and crushed peppercorns in a small, heavy saucepan and bring to a boil. Lower the heat and simmer for 1 minute, or until reduced by one third.

2 Remove from the heat and let cool, then strain the liquid into a heatproof bowl (or in the top of a double boiler over simmering water). Add the egg yolks to the liquid and whisk together.

3 Set the bowl over a pan of simmering water, with the bottom of the bowl just above the water. Whisk the mixture for 5–6 minutes, or until it thickens and becomes creamy, smooth, and ribbon-like in texture.

4 Slowly add the clarified butter in a thin stream and whisk the sauce until it becomes thick and glossy.

5 Add the lemon juice and season with salt and black pepper and a little cayenne.

6 Serve the sauce immediately or keep it warm in a bain-marie (see page 15) for 15–20 minutes. Putting it into a vacuum thermos is also a good way of keeping it warm.

MALTAISE (BLOOD ORANGE) HOLLANDAISE

Replace the lemon juice in the basic hollandaise with the grated zest and juice of 2 blood oranges. I love this sauce with asparagus.

FRENCH classics

Hollandaise variations

MOUSSELINE HOLLANDAISE

Fold in ⅓ cup lightly whipped heavy cream just
before serving. An ideal accompaniment for hot
asparagus or poached fish.

MUSTARD HOLLANDAISE

Add 1 tablespoon Dijon mustard to the finished
sauce. Wonderful served with grilled fish,
vegetables, and chicken.

GINGER HOLLANDAISE

Peel and grate a 1-inch piece of fresh ginger and
heat it with the butter when clarifying, then proceed
as for the main recipe. I love this hollandaise, as the
ginger adds a lively kick. Ideal with fish or shellfish.

CAVIAR HOLLANDAISE

This and the following sauce are for when you really
want to impress. Add 2 tablespoons sevruga caviar
to the finished sauce, and serve with poached fish.

BLACK TRUFFLE HOLLANDAISE

Add 1 tablespoon chopped fresh or canned black
truffles to the finished sauce. Fantastic with fish,
vegetables such as asparagus or artichokes, and
poached eggs.

MIXED PEPPERCORN HOLLANDAISE

Add ½ teaspoon each of lightly crushed green and
pink peppercorns to the finished sauce. Wonderful
with fish, steaks, and duck and lamb cutlets.

BASIL HOLLANDAISE

Add a handful of basil leaves to the finished
sauce. Lovely with fish, shellfish such as crab,
and egg dishes.

**PG tip—repairing
a curdled sauce**
Emulsified sauces such as
hollandaise, béarnaise, and
cold mayonnaise have a certain
notoriety for separating or
curdling. If this happens,
the problem can be rectified
as follows.

Place a fresh egg yolk in a
clean bowl with 1 tablespoon
water and whisk until combined.
Slowly whisk the curdled sauce
into the mixture a little at a time,
ensuring the "new" sauce is
smooth before you add more of
the curdled one. Alternatively,
you can whisk ice water or an
ice cube into the curdled sauce.
In both cases the sauce should
return to its emulsified state.

23

BÉARNAISE

This is essentially a hollandaise sauce made with a reduction of tarragon and shallots. Its unique flavor makes it one of France's most frequently prepared and best-loved sauces. ⊕ *Traditionally served with grilled steak, it is also wonderful with other grilled meats, poultry, and fish.*

makes 1¾ cups

½ ounce fresh tarragon (about 2 7-inch stalks)

2 shallots, chopped

2 tablespoons white wine vinegar

2 tablespoons water

1 teaspoon lightly crushed white peppercorns

4 egg yolks from cage-free eggs

2¼ sticks unsalted butter, clarified (see tip on page 20)

juice of ½ lemon

salt and freshly cracked black pepper

a pinch of cayenne pepper

1 tablespoon chopped chervil leaves

1 Separate the tarragon leaves from the stalks and roughly chop both, keeping them separate. Put the shallots, vinegar, water, crushed peppercorns, and tarragon stalks in a small, heavy pan and bring to a boil. Lower the heat and reduce the liquid to about 2 tablespoons.

2 Remove from the heat and let cool, then strain into the top of a double boiler. Add the egg yolks to the liquid and whisk together.

3 Place the top of the double boiler over simmering water, with the bottom of the pan just above the water. Whisk the yolk mixture for 5–6 minutes, or until it thickens and becomes creamy, smooth, and ribbon-like in texture.

4 Slowly add the clarified butter in a thin stream and whisk the sauce until it becomes thick and glossy.

5 Add the lemon juice, season with salt, black pepper, and cayenne pepper, then add the tarragon leaves and chervil.

6 Serve the sauce immediately or keep it warm in a bain-marie (see page 15) or vacuum thermos.

PG tips
Adding clarified butter
When adding the clarified butter to the eggs in the bowl, you will find it easier if you stabilize the bowl on a dampened dishtowel or balance it over the saucepan to keep it from moving as you whisk in the butter.

Repairing a béarnaise
If your béarnaise separates or curdles, follow the tip given on page 23.

Béarnaise variation
RED PEPPER
BÉARNAISE
Add 3 tablespoons pureed
red pepper (made in a
blender) to the finished
sauce. Wonderful over
a poached egg and with
smoked salmon or crab.

Béarnaise variations

SORREL BÉARNAISE

Replace the chervil and tarragon leaves with ⅔ ounce chopped sorrel leaves in the finished sauce, and omit the tarragon stalks from the vinegar mixture.

MINT BÉARNAISE (paloise)

Replace the tarragon stalks in the main recipe with two 7-inch mint stalks, stripped of their leaves, and add 2 tablespoons chopped mint leaves at the end, to replace the tarragon and chervil leaves. Goes extremely well with lamb or duck breast.

TOMATO BÉARNAISE (choron)

Add 2 tablespoons well-reduced tomato sauce, or tomato paste, to the finished sauce. Fantastic with grilled steak, lamb, chicken, and grilled white fish.

CRÈME FRAÎCHE BÉARNAISE

Add a good spoonful of crème fraîche to the finished sauce, to lighten it. Wonderful with fish or poached asparagus.

HORSERADISH BÉARNAISE

Add 2 tablespoons horseradish to the finished sauce. You can even serve this with traditional roast beef, although it is especially good with grilled steak or grilled salmon.

PG tip—making sauces in a blender

Most chefs—including myself—even in today's mechanical world, prefer to make their emulsified sauces, such as hollandaise, béarnaise, and mayonnaise, by the traditional hand method: that is, a good old bowl and whisk.

This may seem a little unnecessary when a blender does just as good a job and in far less time. It's just a matter of personal taste. In both methods, however, adding the butter or oil too quickly can result in a "split" or curdled sauce. If this happens, never fear, it can be rectified —don't throw in the towel!

Hollandaise—blender method

Follow the recipe on page 20, but add the cooled, strained vinegar liquid to the blender with the egg yolks and salt and pepper. Blitz for a few seconds until mixed.

With the blender on its maximum speed, trickle in the hot butter via the feed tube and blend until light, thick, and fluffy. Add the lemon juice and adjust the seasoning.

Mayonnaise—blender method

Place all the ingredients (see page 30) except the oil and lemon juice in a blender, then blitz for a few seconds. With the blender on its maximum speed, trickle in the oil via the feed tube in a thin, steady stream. Add the lemon juice and adjust the seasoning.

Béarnaise variation

OLIVE BÉARNAISE

Add 2 tablespoons finely
chopped pitted black olives
to the finished sauce.
Particularly good with
grilled steaks.

MAYONNAISE

The eggs in mayonnaise hold the oil in suspension, while vinegar and lemon juice add acidity and flavor. It is one of the most loved of all French sauces, especially when served with poached and fried fish dishes and cold meats. As you can see on the following pages, a well-prepared base sauce opens up many possibilities for delicious variations.

Store-bought mayonnaise is fine for some everyday uses, but nothing beats the freshness of homemade. Some chefs also prefer to use a little olive oil in their recipe, but I find this somewhat detracts from the natural flavor, as certain olive oils are strong-tasting and will overpower the sauce.

makes 1¼ cups

2 egg yolks from cage-free eggs

1 teaspoon Dijon mustard

1 teaspoon white wine vinegar

salt and freshly cracked black pepper

1 cup sunflower or canola oil

2 teaspoons lemon juice

1 Ensure that all the ingredients are at room temperature, in particular the eggs and oil: this makes emulsifying easier.

2 Put the egg yolks, mustard, and vinegar in a mixing bowl. Add a pinch of salt and pepper.

3 Place the bowl on a dampened dishtowel, to keep it steady, and gradually pour in the oil in a thin stream, whisking all the time with the other hand, until it begins to thicken and forms an emulsion.

4 When all the oil has been incorporated and the mayonnaise is thick, stir in the lemon juice and adjust the seasoning to taste.

PG tips

A lighter mayonnaise

For those calorie-conscious among you, mayonnaise can be made with whole egg, producing a lighter, less rich, and healthier version. And for the cholesterol-aware, canola oil (rapeseed oil) contains both omega 3 and omega 6 fatty acids and is one of the most heart-healthy oils around. It's being used increasingly in sauce-making.

Repairing a separated mayonnaise

When a mayonnaise separates, it is mainly due to one of the following: either the oil was added too rapidly at the beginning, or the egg or the oil was too cold. Or it may be that the quantity of oil was too great for the amount of egg using. Ensure all ingredients are brought to room temperature before using.

If your sauce does separate for any reason, place an egg yolk and a little mustard in a bowl, then slowly beat in the curdled sauce, adding it a little at a time. If the problem was that the egg and oil were too cold, as mentioned above, whisking in a little boiling water can sometimes restabilize the sauce.

Mayonnaise variation
SEVILLE SAUCE
Finish the basic mayonnaise
with orange juice instead
of lemon juice and add a
little grated orange zest.
Particularly good with cold
poached asparagus.

Mayonnaise variations

LIGHT MAYONNAISE

Fold ⅓ cup lightly whipped heavy cream into the basic mayonnaise.

GRIBICHE SAUCE

Use hard-boiled egg yolks, pressed through a fine mesh strainer, instead of raw, then proceed as for the basic recipe. Add 1 tablespoon each of rinsed and chopped capers, chopped chervil, and chopped gherkin, with 1 teaspoon Worcestershire sauce, to the finished sauce. Great with fish.

PESTO MAYONNAISE

Add ¼ cup pesto (see page 77) to the basic recipe. Particularly good with cold artichokes or as a dip for vegetable crudités.

TYROLIENNE SAUCE

Add 2 tablespoons tomato paste, ½ teaspoon hot chili sauce, and a small quantity of chopped fresh herbs to the basic recipe. Great with fried fish or cold poultry.

AIOLI

Add 4 crushed garlic cloves to the egg yolks at the start, then proceed as for the basic recipe. A little pureed cooked potato may also be added to the egg yolks at this stage. Fantastic for hot or cold fish or as a dip for vegetables, bread, and so on.

ROUILLE SAUCE

Add a pinch of saffron threads, 1 teaspoon tomato paste, 1 finely chopped red chile, and ¼ teaspoon cayenne pepper to the basic recipe. Traditionally served with bouillabaisse or other fish soups, but also great with fried fish.

AVOCADO SAUCE

Add to the basic recipe ½ peeled avocado, blended in a food processor with 1 teaspoon lemon juice. Fantastic with cold poached salmon.

FENNEL MAYONNAISE

Add 2 tablespoons chopped fennel fronds, or dill, and 2 teaspoons anise liquor, such as Pernod, to the basic recipe.

TARTAR SAUCE

Add to the basic recipe 1 tablespoon each of finely chopped gherkins, rinsed and chopped capers, chopped flat-leaf parsley and chervil, and chopped shallots. Traditionally served with deep- or pan-fried fish.

RÉMOULADE SAUCE

Add 1 teaspoon finely chopped canned anchovy fillet and 2 tablespoons chopped tarragon to the tartar sauce recipe above. Serve with cold meats, cold fish, and fried fish.

RED WINE MAYONNAISE

Put 1 cup good red wine, a sprig of thyme, and a little cracked black pepper in a pan and reduce to a syrup. Add 1 tablespoon red currant jelly, strain, then set aside to cool completely. Stir this into the basic mayonnaise recipe and serve with cold meat, especially roast beef.

CURRY MAYONNAISE (sauce indienne)

Add 1 tablespoon mild curry powder to the basic recipe.

THOUSAND ISLAND SAUCE

Add to the basic recipe 3 tablespoons tomato ketchup, 1 tablespoon chopped shallot, and ½ tablespoon each of chopped red and green pepper.

GREEN SAUCE (sauce verte)

Put ½ cup pureed cooked spinach, a bunch of watercress, and 1 tablespoon each of chopped chervil, tarragon, and chives in a blender. Blitz, then add to the basic recipe.

WARM BUTTER SAUCES

These are also known as white butter sauces or beurre blanc—a hot sauce based on wine and vinegar, reduced with shallots, finished with butter, then whipped until smooth. Traditionally served with fish dishes.

BEURRE BLANC

This is another style of warm, emulsified butter sauce, thought to have come about by accident at the end of the 19th century, when a French cook to the aristocracy forgot to include the eggs in a béarnaise. It is rich in flavor, simple to prepare, and stands proudly alongside the other two classic warm butter sauces, hollandaise and béarnaise.

makes 1¼ cups

2 shallots, finely chopped
3 tablespoons white wine vinegar
¼ cup dry white wine
2 tablespoons cold water
1¾ sticks unsalted butter, chilled and cubed
salt and freshly cracked black pepper
a squeeze of lemon juice

1 Put the shallots, vinegar, and white wine in a small pan and bring to a boil. Lower the heat and reduce for about 2 minutes, to about 1 tablespoon; it should have a syrupy consistency.
2 Over a gentle heat, add the water, then whisk in the butter a little at a time until emulsified.
3 Add salt, pepper, and lemon juice to taste. For a smooth sauce, strain it to remove the shallots.

PG tip A spoonful or two of heavy cream added to the wine reduction helps stabilize the sauce if you need to keep it for a length of time, but it does tend to lose some of its buttery flavor.

Variations

NANTAIS BUTTER

This first, often interchangeable, cousin of the beurre blanc sauce is made with equal amounts of wine and wine vinegar, giving the sauce a more acidic flavor. Increase the white wine vinegar in the main recipe to ¼ cup and reduce the mixture to 2 tablespoons. Great with oily fish.

BASIL BEURRE BLANC

Add 2 tablespoons chopped basil to the finished sauce.

HERB BEURRE BLANC

A lovely, fresh-tasting sauce. Add 3 tablespoons of your favorite herb: tarragon, chervil, and parsley are particularly good.

ROSÉ WINE BEURRE BLANC

The wine adds a lovely red tinge to the butter sauce. Replace the white wine with rosé wine and the vinegar with red wine vinegar. Finish with a spoonful of reduced meat stock (optional).

SOY AND TOMATO BEURRE BLANC

Add 1 tablespoon light soy sauce and 5 tablespoons reduced tomato sauce to the reduction before whisking in the butter. Before serving, strain the sauce through a fine mesh strainer. Wonderful with salmon or scallops.

SAFFRON BEURRE BLANC

Add a pinch of saffron threads to the reduction before whisking in the butter, then proceed as for the basic recipe.

GINGER AND LEMON BEURRE BLANC

Add 1 tablespoon grated fresh ginger to the reduction before whisking in the butter, then proceed as for the basic recipe. Finish with 1 teaspoon grated lemon zest. Great with oily fish, such as salmon.

WATERCRESS BEURRE BLANC

Puree a bunch of watercress and add to the finished sauce, then strain it to give a wonderful, green, fresh-tasting butter.

Other warm butter sauces

Below is a list of other simple butter-based sauces on similar lines:

BEURRE NOISETTE (brown butter sauce)

Heat ¾ stick salted butter in a frying pan over a medium-high heat for 1–2 minutes, or until it foams up and becomes golden and nutty brown. Add a squeeze of lemon juice, then pour it over pan-fried fish or vegetables.

BEURRE NOIR (black butter sauce)

Prepare as for brown butter sauce (above), but cook the butter for 20–30 seconds longer, or until it takes on a dark color. Traditionally served with pan-fried skate and capers.

BEURRE FONDU (drawn butter sauce)

Bring ¼ cup water to a boil, then whisk in 1¼ sticks cubed, chilled, salted butter until emulsified. Finish with a squeeze of lemon. Most commonly served with asparagus, alongside or instead of hollandaise, it is sometimes also used to reheat vegetables ready for serving.

COMPOUND BUTTERS

Also known as hard butter sauces, these cold, flavored butter sauces may also be sweetened, to serve over warm desserts (see page 218). Their beauty is that they can be prepared well in advance and kept in the fridge or freezer until needed.

There are some important tips to remember when making these sauces: ensure the butter is at room temperature and soft before beating; ensure the flavoring ingredients are chopped small before adding them to the butter; and finally make sure you let the butter stand for 30 minutes prior to rolling in the paper, to allow the flavors to permeate.

MAÎTRE D'HÔTEL BUTTER (parsley butter)

⊕ *The most popular of the cold butter sauces, served with grilled fish, steaks, or vegetables.* For a variation, you can replace the parsley with other herbs of your choice, such as tarragon, basil, or thyme.

1¾ sticks good-quality unsalted butter, softened
salt and freshly cracked black pepper
a pinch of paprika
3 tablespoons chopped flat-leaf parsley
juice of ¼ lemon

1 Put the softened butter in a bowl and season with salt, pepper, and paprika.
2 Add the parsley and lemon juice and beat together well.
3 Let it stand for 30 minutes, then roll the butter in waxed paper or foil into a sausage shape, twist the ends, and tighten to form a bon-bon shape. Chill in the fridge or freezer until needed.
4 To serve, remove the butter from its paper roll, let it soften slightly for 2–3 minutes, then cut into slices about ½-inch thick. Place the butter on your piece of cooked meat or fish and it will melt slowly over the food—delicious!

Variations
SHELLFISH BUTTER

Substitute ¾ cup finely chopped peeled cooked shrimp, shelled cooked lobster or crayfish for the parsley. Mix in 1 teaspoon tomato paste, a good dash of cognac, and the juice of another ¼ lemon. Great with fish and shellfish.

MERLOT BUTTER

Put ⅓ cup good merlot wine and a finely chopped shallot in a pan and reduce to 2 tablespoons. Add to the butter in place of the paprika, parsley, and lemon juice. Wonderful with grilled steaks.

ROQUEFORT BUTTER

Add ½ cup crumbled Roquefort cheese in place of the paprika, parsley, and lemon juice. Ideal with grilled steak and lamb or pork chops.

PORCINI BUTTER

Soak ⅓ ounce dried porcini mushrooms in a mixture of ⅔ cup water and ¼ cup Madeira for 1 hour. Place in a pan, simmer for 5 minutes, then remove the mushrooms and let them cool. Reduce the liquid to a syrup, strain, and let cool. Chop the mushrooms finely and add them, along with the reduced liquid, to the butter in the main recipe, in place of the paprika, parsley, and lemon juice.

ESCARGOT BUTTER

Add 1 teaspoon crushed garlic, use only 2 tablespoons parsley, and omit the paprika and lemon juice. Traditionally served with snails, vegetables, or grilled meats. You can try using smoked garlic here for an interesting variation.

FOIE GRAS BUTTER

Add ¼ cup pureed foie gras pâté and 2 tablespoons Madeira in place of the paprika, parsley, and lemon juice. Good with grilled meats and game.

SMOKED PAPRIKA BUTTER

Add 1 teaspoon smoked paprika to the butter in place of the parsley and lemon juice. Wonderful with grilled meats and fish.

CAFÉ DE PARIS BUTTER

Replace the parsley and lemon juice with 2 tablespoons tomato ketchup, 1 teaspoon Dijon mustard, ½ teaspoon chopped rinsed capers, 1 chopped shallot, 2 finely chopped, rinsed canned anchovy fillets, and 1 teaspoon each of chives and tarragon. Mix well, then stir in a dash of Madeira or cognac. Great with grilled meats.

GRAINY MUSTARD BUTTER

Add 1 teaspoon grainy mustard in place of the paprika and lemon juice, using just 2 tablespoons parsley. Goes well with grilled fish, seafood, and meat, and game dishes.

FENNEL AND SAFFRON BUTTER

Infuse a good pinch of saffron threads in ¼ cup water. Add this to the butter in the basic recipe along with ½ teaspoon toasted fennel seeds in place of the paprika, parsley, and lemon juice. Wonderful with seafood, especially scallops.

STEAK BUTTER

Replace the parsley and lemon juice with 4 very finely chopped canned anchovies or 1 teaspoon anchovy paste. Traditionally served as an accompaniment to steaks in gentlemen's clubs.

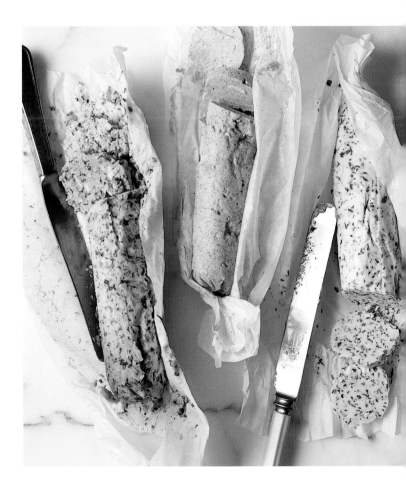

WHITE SAUCES

Béchamel is the name for the classic white sauce made from milk and a white-based roux. It forms the base of many great sauces, such as the famous cheese sauce, mornay. When correctly made, a good béchamel will be smooth and creamy in appearance, rather than thick and pasty. Like many of the great French classic sauces, béchamel is often replaced in restaurant kitchens nowadays by a sauce made completely of rich cream, and sometimes a classically made béchamel is finished with a spoonful or two of cream.

BÉCHAMEL

The onion studded with cloves adds extra flavor to the milk base.

makes 2½ cups

1 small onion, cut in half

4 whole cloves

2½ cups whole milk

1 small bay leaf

3 tablespoons unsalted butter

3 tablespoons all-purpose flour

a little salt and freshly cracked black pepper

a little freshly grated nutmeg

¼ cup heavy cream (optional)

1 Stud each onion half with 2 cloves, then place in a pan with the milk and bay leaf. Bring to a boil and simmer gently for 4–5 minutes, to infuse.

2 In another pan, melt the butter, add the flour, and cook for 30–40 seconds, stirring frequently with a wooden spoon, until the roux is pale yellow.

3 Strain the milk through a fine strainer, then beat it vigorously into the roux, until the sauce is smooth and silky in appearance.

4 Slowly bring the béchamel to a boil, reduce the heat, then simmer for 20 minutes, beating occasionally, until the sauce is smooth and glossy.

5 Season with salt, pepper, and nutmeg and stir in the cream, if using.

PG tip If you are in a hurry, you can adopt the all-in-one method: do not infuse the milk, but instead put all the ingredients (omitting the onion, cloves and bay leaf) in a pan over a low heat and stir continuously until the sauce boils and thickens. Keep stirring for 3–4 minutes. Season with salt, pepper, and nutmeg, and add the cream, if using.

Béchamel variations

MORNAY SAUCE (cheese sauce)

Classically made with Gruyère or another Swiss cheese, this is great for coating vegetables such as cauliflower, leeks, and broccoli. Simply remove the béchamel sauce from the heat and add 1 cup grated Gruyère or cheddar, and 1 teaspoon Dijon mustard. Stir in 2 egg yolks from cage-free eggs, mixed with ¼ cup lightly whipped cream.

EGG AND MUSTARD SAUCE

Add 2 teaspoons Dijon mustard and 2 tablespoons each of light cream, roughly chopped hard-boiled cage-free eggs, and roughly chopped flat-leaf parsley to the finished sauce. Lovely served over poached fish, especially haddock or plaice.

CAPER SAUCE

Add ⅓ cup well-rinsed and roughly chopped superfine capers and the juice of ¼ lemon to the finished sauce. Great with a boiled leg of lamb or mutton. If you are serving lamb with this, add ⅔ cup of the poaching lamb liquor as well.

SOUBISE SAUCE

Blanch 2 chopped large onions or 4 chopped shallots in boiling water for 2 minutes, then drain and sauté them in 3½ tablespoons unsalted butter until very soft but not browned. Add these to the basic sauce recipe along with a pinch of sugar and cook, stirring, for 15–20 minutes. Blitz in a blender until smooth, then stir in ⅓ cup heavy cream. Superb with lamb or pork.

GOOSEBERRY SAUCE

This sauce I first came across as a trainee in the West Country of England: a local classic served with grilled mackerel, it remains one of my favorites to this day. Poach 1 cup fresh gooseberries in ⅓ cup water along with 2 tablespoons granulated sugar for 15 minutes, then add the béchamel from the basic recipe and cook for 2–3 minutes. Transfer to a blender and blitz until smooth and creamy, or use an immersion blender.

VELOUTÉ

Made in the same way as béchamel, velouté is a smooth, velvety sauce made using a white roux and a flavored white stock (veal, chicken, or fish). It is vitally important that the stock is of the highest quality, to obtain the best results. Many chefs have abandoned the classic velouté in favor of a sauce made from stock with reduced cream and flavorings, as a matter of convenience and flavor. Below are recipes for both versions.

CLASSIC VELOUTÉ

makes 2½ cups

4 cups well-flavored chicken, veal, or fish stock
   (see pages 8–9)
¼ cup (½ stick) unsalted butter
¼ cup all-purpose plain flour
salt and freshly cracked black pepper

1 Bring the stock to a boil. In another pan, melt the butter, add the flour, and stir to make a white roux.

2 Stir in the stock with a wooden spoon, then change to a whisk and bring the mixture to a boil. Skim off any impurities that form on the surface.

3 Simmer over a low heat until reduced by one third, then strain.

MODERN VELOUTÉ

The reduction of wine, along with the aromatics, produces a richer sauce than the classic version given on the left.

makes 2½ cups

4 shallots, chopped
a little fresh thyme if using chicken or veal
   stock, or 1 cup chopped button mushrooms
   if using fish
1 tablespoon unsalted butter
1¼ cups dry white wine
1¾ cups well-flavored chicken, veal, or fish stock
   (see pages 8–9)
1½ cups heavy cream

1 In a pan, sweat the shallots and thyme or mushrooms in the butter until softened. Add the wine and bring to a boil.

2 Reduce the heat and simmer for 20–25 minutes, or until the liquid has reduced by two thirds and is syrupy in consistency.

3 Add the stock, return the mixture to a boil, and cook over a high heat for another 20 minutes, or until reduced by half. Add the cream, return it to a boil, then lower the heat and simmer until it has reduced by half again; it should have thickened enough to coat the back of a spoon. Strain the sauce before using.

Velouté variations

Choose your type of stock to match the dish you are serving.

AURORE (tomato velouté)

Add ⅓ cup fresh tomato sauce (see page 58) or passata to the finished sauce. Great with poached chicken, crab, or lobster.

HERB VELOUTÉ

Add 2 tablespoons of your favorite herb to the finished sauce; I like a mixture of chervil, tarragon, and chives. Lovely with poached fish, shellfish, and white meat dishes.

ANCHOVY AND MUSTARD VELOUTÉ

Add 1 teaspoon Dijon mustard and 1 teaspoon anchovy paste to the finished sauce. Good with poached fish, especially sole or halibut.

WILD MUSHROOM VELOUTÉ

Add ½ cup sautéed wild mushrooms to the finished sauce, or ⅓ ounce dried mushrooms presoaked in water (enough to cover) for 1 hour and added to the basic sauce along with the soaking liquid. If you prefer a smooth sauce, transfer the sauce to a blender and blitz until smooth.

SHELLFISH VELOUTÉ

Velouté can also be made using the cooking juices of poached shellfish such as mussels or clams instead of the stock. The shellfish is generally added to the sauce for serving.

Velouté variation

SAFFRON VELOUTÉ

Add a good pinch of saffron threads to ¼ cup boiling stock or water, then add to the finished sauce. Serve with fish or shellfish, such as poached scallops —delicious! I often also add some chopped tomato and basil.

BROWN SAUCES

LIGHTLY THICKENED VEAL JUS

In days gone by, this brown sauce was known as a "demi-glace" (half glaze)—once the mainstay of classic French cuisine. It took the best part of two days to prepare, and formed the base of many of the famous classic brown sauces. Today it has all but vanished in favor of a lighter sauce called a "jus" (juices). This jus can be made with meat, poultry, game, fish, and vegetables, and produces a clearer, more refined and certainly less time-consuming sauce. It should be thick and glossy, and should lightly coat the back of a spoon.

makes 2½ cups

3 tablespoons vegetable oil

¾ pound veal trimmings (see PG tip, below)

5 ounces chicken wings, roughly chopped into
    small pieces

4 shallots, chopped

1 cup mushrooms or mushroom trimmings
    and peelings

1 carrot, roughly chopped

1 garlic clove, crushed

½ tablespoon tomato paste

a small sprig of thyme

1 small bay leaf

1¼ cups dry white wine

2½ cups water

6 cups veal, beef, or dark chicken stock
    (see page 9)

1 tablespoon arrowroot, mixed with a little water

PG tip Since veal can be hard to obtain as well as expensive, beef trimmings can be used instead.

1 Heat the oil in a large pan and, when it is very hot, add the meat pieces. Fry over a high heat for about 20 minutes, moving the pieces around until they are golden brown all over.

2 Add the vegetables and garlic and continue to fry for another 10 minutes, until golden and caramelized. Add the tomato paste, thyme, and bay leaf, and cook for 2–3 minutes more.

3 Add the wine and water and bring to a boil, scraping the sediment from the pan with a wooden spoon to release the caramelized juices.

4 Cook, uncovered, for 20 minutes, to reduce by two thirds. Add the stock and return to a boil, then simmer for 20–25 minutes to reduce by half again, skimming to remove any impurities.

5 Stir in the arrowroot and mix to thicken the liquid. Cook for 2 minutes, then strain through a fine mesh strainer.

LIGHTLY THICKENED POULTRY JUS

Follow the recipe above for lightly thickened veal jus, but substitute chicken wings or duck bones for the veal trimmings. Made this way, it is light and delicate—perfect for chicken dishes or braising vegetables. The jus-based sauces below are ideally made with a base of veal jus, but chicken can be used if you prefer.

Jus-based brown sauces

BORDELAISE SAUCE

One of the great French sauces for sautéed steaks or roast beef. Place 3 finely chopped shallots, 1 cup red wine, a sprig of thyme, 6 crushed black peppercorns, and a small bay leaf in a pan, bring to a boil, and reduce by half. Add 1¼ cups jus, then simmer, uncovered, for 10 minutes. Strain through a fine mesh strainer, then add 2 ounces cleaned bone marrow (soaked in warm water for 5 minutes). Drain, whisk in a pat of chilled butter, and season to taste.

Brown sauce variation

DEVILED SAUCE

Bring 3 chopped shallots, 6 crushed black peppercorns, 1 bay leaf, a sprig of thyme, ⅓ cup dry white wine, and 5 tablespoons white wine vinegar to a boil. Reduce by half, add 1¼ cups veal jus and simmer, uncovered, for 10 minutes. Strain, stir in 1 tablespoon Worcestershire sauce and a pat of chilled butter, then season to taste. Great with grilled chicken or calf's liver.

CHATEAUBRIAND SAUCE

Another great steak-inspired sauce. Cook
3 chopped shallots, a few mushroom trimmings,
a little thyme, and 1 bay leaf in butter until
golden. Add ⅓ cup dry white wine, then simmer,
uncovered, for 10 minutes. Add a scant cup jus
and cook for another 5 minutes. Strain through a
fine mesh strainer. Reheat to serve, then whisk in
3½ tablespoons maître d'hôtel butter (page 36)
and 1 tablespoon tarragon. Season to taste.

ROBERT SAUCE

One of the greats; the mustard adds a real kick.
It is traditionally served with pork, but I enjoy it
with chicken, too. Or for a variation, also good
with pork, add some finely chopped gherkins to
create sauce charcutière. For Robert Sauce, heat
1 tablespoon unsalted butter in a small pan, add
1 small onion, finely chopped, and cook over a
low heat for 8–10 minutes, until cooked but
not colored. Pour in ⅓ cup dry white wine and
2 tablespoons white wine vinegar and reduce by
half. Add 1¼ cups jus and cook for 15 minutes.
Strain, pressing down on the onions for maximum
flavor. Heat the mixture, stir in 3 teaspoons Dijon
mustard and another tablespoon of butter, season
to taste and serve.

POIVRADE SAUCE

A light, peppery-flavored sauce. Sweat 1 crushed
garlic clove, 1 chopped shallot, 1 chopped small
carrot, and 1 chopped stick of celery in 2 teaspoons
unsalted butter. Add a scant cap red wine,
5 tablespoons red wine vinegar, a sprig of thyme,
and 1 small bay leaf, and cook, uncovered, for 10
minutes. Add 12 lightly crushed black peppercorns
and a scant cup veal jus and simmer for 5 minutes,
then strain through a fine mesh strainer. Whisk in a
good pat of chilled butter and season to taste.

REFORM SAUCE

Perhaps my all-time favorite: I love its hot and
sweet flavor. Sweat 2 chopped shallots in a little
butter, add ⅔ cup red wine, and reduce by half.
Add a scant cup jus and reduce by half again. Stir in
2 tablespoons red currant jelly, strain, whisk in a pat
of chilled butter, and season to taste. Serve with
lamb cutlets cooked in a crispy crumb crust.

TAPENADE

Wonderful with lamb or duck breast. Sweat
some shallots in a little butter. Add ⅓ cup dry white
wine and cook, uncovered, for 5 minutes. Add
1 cup veal jus and cook for 10 minutes. Add
2 tablespoons tapenade (see page 74), whisk in a
good pat of chilled butter, then season to taste.

FORTIFIED WINE-BASED JUS

Heat a scant cup prepared jus with ⅓ cup Madeira,
port, or Marsala. Cook for 5 minutes, then whisk in
a good pat of chilled butter and season to taste.

PÉRIGOURDINE SAUCE

For real extravagance, heat ⅔ cup Madeira-fortified
jus (see above), then add 1 tablespoon chopped
fresh or canned truffles. Simmer for 2–3 minutes,
whisk in a pat of butter and season to taste.

GAME JUS

This hearty sauce is used as a base sauce for furred and feathered game dishes. Although it is fair to say that most people do not prepare game at home, I thought it worthwhile including it here anyway, for the few who do.

makes about 3 cups

2 tablespoons vegetable oil

1 pound, 10 ounces game trimmings, cut into
    small pieces

2 tablespoons unsalted butter

2 carrots, chopped

1 onion, chopped

a sprig of thyme

1 bay leaf

10 black peppercorns, lightly crushed

2 tablespoons red wine vinegar

2½ tablespoons flour

⅔ cup red wine

2½ cups game or veal stock (see page 9)

2½ cups water

½ teaspoon juniper berries

1 Heat the oil in a large, heavy pan. Add the game trimmings and fry until golden, about 20 minutes. Add the butter, vegetables, herbs, and peppercorns, and fry until caramelized.

2 Add the vinegar and heat for 1 minute. Add the flour, mix well, and cook over a low heat for 5 minutes. Pour in the wine, stock, and water, then bring to a boil, skimming off any impurities that rise to the surface.

3 Add the juniper berries and simmer, uncovered, for 45 minutes, skimming regularly. Strain through a fine mesh strainer.

Variations

The very traditional sauces below are variations on the above game jus, and follow classic French principles. They have a great affinity with strong, rich game such as venison or hare.

GAME POIVRADE SAUCE

Put ¼ cup red currant jelly with 1 tablespoon crushed black peppercorns and ⅓ cup red wine in a pan. Cook over medium heat until reduced and syrupy, about 3–4 minutes. Add the game jus and strain, then finish with ⅓ cup port.

GRAND-VENEUR SAUCE

Follow the poivrade recipe above, but add ⅓ cup heavy cream and a pat of unsalted butter with the port, and whisk into the warm sauce before serving.

SALMIS SAUCE

For a wonderfully rich and caramelized flavor, add ⅓ cup truffle juice and ⅔ cup good-quality sherry to the finished game jus.

PAN SAUCES AND GRAVIES

Pan sauces are in essence one of the simplest ways available to the cook for making a sauce. They are made from the caramelized juices left behind by pan-fried meat, poultry, or fish, and you make the sauce there and then in the flameproof pan, while the meat is resting somewhere else. This method of sauce-making is known as "deglazing," which simply means the pan juices are swilled with a liquid—usually wine, stock, cream, or meat jus—to dislodge any caramelized pieces.

Gravies are made from the meat juices left in a pan after roasting or frying. Any excess fat is normally removed before wine or stock is added. Sometimes flour is mixed into the fat and browned for a few minutes before the liquid is added, resulting in a thicker gravy. Some chefs thicken their gravies by adding a little beurre manié (see page 12), or by reducing the stock down in the pan until it thickens naturally.

Here are a few of my favorite pan sauce and gravy recipes.

SAUTÉED CORN-FED CHICKEN CHASSEUR

serves 4

2 tablespoons vegetable oil

1 tablespoon unsalted butter

1 corn-fed chicken, about 3½ pounds, cut up

salt and freshly cracked black pepper

⅓ cup dry white wine

1 cup button mushrooms, sliced

14½-ounce can tomatoes, chopped

2 tablespoons chopped tarragon leaves

⅔ cup lightly thickened chicken jus (see page 44)

1 Heat the oil and butter in a heavy frying pan. Season the chicken pieces liberally with salt and pepper and add them to the pan.

2 Fry the chicken until golden all over and cooked through, about 8–10 minutes. Remove to a plate and keep warm.

3 Deglaze the pan with the wine and boil for 1 minute, stirring up the caramelized cooking juices, before adding the mushrooms, tomatoes, and tarragon.

4 Cook for 5 minutes to infuse the flavors. Add the chicken jus to the pan and cook for 2 minutes more.

5 Pour the sauce over the chicken and serve.

ENTRECÔTE "BALSAMIC AU POIVRE"

A little balsamic vinegar added to the classic version of steak au poivre produces something a bit different.

serves 4

1 teaspoon black peppercorns, lightly crushed

2 teaspoons drained green peppercorns in brine, rinsed

4 entrecôte (sirloin) steaks, 7 ounces each

2 tablespoons vegetable oil

1 tablespoon unsalted butter

1 tablespoon balsamic vinegar

2 tablespoons brandy

⅓ cup lightly thickened veal jus (see page 44)

3 tablespoons heavy cream

salt and freshly cracked black pepper

1 Mix the black and green peppercorns together and lightly press them onto the surface of both sides of the steaks.

2 Heat the oil and butter in a heavy frying pan and add the steaks. Cook them on both sides to your liking: 2–3 minutes each side for rare; 4–5 minutes each side for medium, and 7–8 minutes per side for well-done. Remove to a plate, cover with foil, and keep warm.

3 Deglaze the pan with the balsamic vinegar and brandy and simmer for 1 minute, stirring up the caramelized cooking juices as the liquid reduces.

4 Add the veal jus and cream, and cook for 2–3 minutes, until the sauce is thick enough to coat the back of a spoon.

5 Season with salt and pepper, then pour the sauce over the steaks and serve.

CALF'S LIVER VÉNITIENNE

⊕ *This sauce is good not only with liver but delicious with pork and beef, too, or served over creamy mashed potatoes.*

serves 4

2 tablespoons vegetable oil

2 tablespoons unsalted butter

8 thin slices of calf's liver, 3 ounces each

1 onion, very thinly sliced

8 sage leaves, roughly chopped

⅓ cup dry white wine

¼ cup Marsala

⅓ cup lightly thickened veal jus (see page 44)

salt and freshly cracked black pepper

1 Heat the oil with 1 tablespoon of the butter in a heavy frying pan. When it is very hot, add the liver slices, in batches, and fry for 2½ minutes on each side. Remove to a plate, cover with foil, and keep warm.

2 Add the onion and sage and fry until the onion is lightly golden and softened, about 3–4 minutes.

3 Deglaze the pan with the wine, stirring up the caramelized cooking juices.

4 Add the Marsala and veal jus and boil for 2–3 minutes. Season to taste, then whisk the remaining butter into the sauce and serve it poured over the liver.

BASIC ROAST GRAVIES

🌐 *This recipe is suitable for any sort of roast, whether meat, poultry, or game.* Ideally you should use the appropriate stock for enhancing the gravy: lamb stock for roast lamb, chicken stock for roast chicken, and so on.

makes 2½ cups

3 tablespoons flour

2½ cups well-flavored hot stock, the type according to the roast (see page 9)

salt and freshly cracked black pepper

1 After roasting the meat, remove to a warmed plate and set aside to rest. Remove the excess fat from the roasting pan, leaving about 2 tablespoons.

2 Over the heat, and using a wooden spoon, scrape up the caramelized pan juices, then add the flour, blending it well into the fat and juices.

3 Cook for 2 minutes until the flour becomes a light golden color.

4 Add the stock and bring to a boil, stirring constantly. Boil until the sauce thickens and is reduced by a third.

5 Season to taste, then strain through a fine mesh strainer and serve.

Variations

HERB AND MUSTARD GRAVY

Simply add a small handful of your favorite herbs to the reducing gravy, such as rosemary, thyme, or sage. Whisk in 1 tablespoon Dijon mustard before straining.

WINE-INFUSED GRAVY

Substitute ⅓ cup red wine, port, or white wine for ⅓ cup of the stock and add gradually as for the stock.

BEER GRAVY

Add a 12-ounce bottle of dark beer to the gravy in place of 1½ cups of the stock. Wonderful with roast beef or pork.

VEGETABLE-BASED SAUCES

Vegetable sauces add not only color to a dish but a touch of freshness as well—ideal for vegetarian (using vegetable stock, of course) and light dishes. This type of sauce, which derives its body either entirely or in part from pureed vegetables, is often referred to as a coulis (see also fruit coulis, page 211). As a rough guide, the quantities here are generally enough for eight servings, although this will depend upon how you are using each one, and with what.

SWEET PEPPER SAUCE

⊕ *Great with steamed fish, pasta, and vegetables.*

makes 2 cups

2 red, green, or yellow peppers, seeded and
  chopped
3 tablespoons unsalted butter
a generous pinch of sugar
scant cup vegetable stock (see page 10) or water
a sprig of thyme
⅓ cup heavy cream
salt and freshly cracked black pepper

1 Put the chopped peppers in a pan with
1 tablespoon of the butter and the pinch of sugar.
2 Cover with a lid and let it sweat over a low heat
until the peppers begin to soften. Add the stock or
water, and thyme, and bring to a boil.
3 Reduce the heat, then simmer gently, uncovered,
for 15–20 minutes.
4 Discard the thyme and transfer the mixture to a
blender. Blitz to a puree, then strain back into the
pan through a fine mesh strainer.
5 Reheat the sauce and whisk in the cream and the
remaining butter. Season to taste.

GARDEN PEA AND MINT SAUCE

⊕ *Great with poached salmon or poached or steamed asparagus. It is also very good over goat cheese ravioli. For a variation, you can replace the mint with basil.*

makes 2 cups

1¼ cups white chicken or vegetable stock
  (see pages 8 and 10)
1 cup podded fresh peas (or frozen)
a small handful of mint leaves
¼ cup light cream
2 teaspoons unsalted butter
salt and freshly cracked black pepper

1 Put the stock in a pan and bring to a boil. Add the
peas and mint leaves and return to a boil.
2 Cook for 5–6 minutes for fresh peas or 2 minutes
for frozen peas, then transfer the mixture to a
blender. Blitz until smooth, then strain back into
the pan through a fine mesh strainer.
3 Reheat the sauce and add the cream. Whisk in
the butter and season to taste.

PUMPKIN SAUCE

⊕ *I had to include this sauce as it is so good served with seasonal wild mushrooms or with pasta. A must for the autumn season.*

makes about 3 cups

2 tablespoons olive oil

2 tablespoons unsalted butter

¾ pound peeled and seeded pumpkin, cut into ¾-inch pieces

2 shallots, finely chopped

1 garlic clove, crushed

2 cups light chicken or vegetable stock (see pages 8 and 10)

⅓ cup light cream

a pinch of ground cinnamon

salt and freshly cracked black pepper

1 Heat the oil and 1½ tablespoons of the butter in a pan, add the pumpkin pieces, and cover. Cook for 5 minutes over medium heat, until softened and lightly caramelized.

2 Add the shallots and garlic and cook for 2–3 minutes more.

3 Add the stock and boil for 8–10 minutes.

4 Transfer the mixture to a blender and blitz until smooth. Strain back into the pan through a fine mesh strainer.

5 Whisk in the cream and remaining butter and bring to a boil, still whisking. Add the cinnamon and season with salt and pepper.

SHALLOT TARTS WITH WILD MUSHROOMS AND PUMPKIN SAUCE

serves 4

12 ounces small shallots

¾ cup sugar

2 tablespoons unsalted butter

⅓ cup sherry vinegar

½ teaspoon thyme leaves

12 ounces prepared puff pastry dough (fresh or frozen), thinly rolled

8-ounce selection of wild mushrooms

2 tablespoons olive oil

salt and freshly cracked black pepper

½ quantity of pumpkin sauce (see left), heated

1 Blanch the shallots in boiling water for 4–5 minutes, then drain and let cool.

2 Put the sugar in a nonstick frying pan and heat, stirring constantly until the sugar caramelizes.

3 Add 1½ tablespoons of the butter and stir into the caramel.

4 Add the blanched shallots, sherry vinegar, and thyme, and continue cooking until the caramel completely coats the shallots and the shallots are soft and cooked through. Transfer to a bowl and let cool.

5 Preheat the oven to 350°F. When the shallot mixture is cool, divide it between 4 tart pans, 3½–4 inches in diameter, and place on a baking sheet.

6 Stamp out 4 circles, 3½–4 inches in diameter, from the rolled dough and lay one over each shallot-filled tart pan, pressing around the edges to seal.

7 Melt the remaining butter and brush the tops of the tarts. Transfer to the oven and bake for 15–20 minutes.

8 Meanwhile, sauté the mushrooms in a hot pan with the olive oil, then season well and keep warm.

9 Turn out the tarts, shallot-side up, onto 4 serving plates. Top each with the wild mushrooms, pour the pumpkin sauce around them, and serve.

PORCINI CREAM SAUCE

If you wish to use fresh porcini, replace the dried with 6 ounces (2½ cups) washed and chopped fresh ones, cooked in a little butter at the beginning of the recipe.

⊕ *Great with veal or chicken, or added to a mushroom risotto, gnocchi, or pasta.*

makes 1¼ cups

⅓ ounce dried porcini mushrooms

⅔ cup hot chicken or vegetable stock
   (see pages 8 and 10)

2 tablespoons unsalted butter

2 shallots, chopped

3½ tablespoons port

3½ tablespoons Madeira

¼ cup heavy cream

3 tablespoons lightly thickened chicken jus
   (see page 44; optional)

salt and freshly cracked black pepper

1 Soak the porcini in the stock for 30 minutes, then strain, reserving the soaking liquid and the porcini separately.

2 Heat 1 tablespoon of the butter in a pan and add the soaked porcini and shallots. Cover and sweat for 5 minutes over a low heat.

3 Add the port, Madeira, and reserved stock, and bring to a boil. Cook for 2–3 minutes.

4 Transfer the mixture to a blender and blitz until smooth, then strain back into the pan through a fine mesh strainer.

5 Add the cream and chicken jus, if using, and cook for 3–4 minutes. Whisk in the remaining butter, season to taste, and serve.

ASPARAGUS AND LEMON SAUCE

⊕ *I often add 1–2 chopped sticks of lemongrass, to the stock, along with the asparagus peelings. With or without this addition, the sauce is wonderful served with fish or shellfish, such as lobster or scallops, or with buttered baby leeks and morels.*

makes 2 cups

11 ounces asparagus spears, trimmed (keep the
   trimmings) and chopped

1 cup white chicken or vegetable stock
   (see pages 8 and 10)

1½ tablespoons unsalted butter

¼ cup heavy cream

½ teaspoon finely grated lemon zest

salt and freshly cracked black pepper

1 Put the asparagus trimmings in a pan with the stock and simmer for 10–15 minutes to infuse, then strain, reserving only the stock.

2 Heat half the butter in a pan, then add the asparagus and cook, covered, for 5 minutes.

3 Add the infused stock and boil for 5–8 minutes until the asparagus is soft.

4 Add the cream and cook for 2 minutes more. Transfer to a blender and blitz until smooth.

5 Strain the sauce back into the pan through a fine mesh strainer and, over the heat, whisk in the remaining butter and the lemon zest. Season to taste.

MISCELLANEOUS SAUCES

An independent group of sauces that form the basis of many great dishes in French cuisine.

RED-WINE-FLAVORED FISH JUS

This sauce has something of the professional kitchen about it, but is easy to make at home.

⊕ *It's lovely with pan-roasted fish or used as a base to braise firm-fleshed fish, such as monkfish (angler fish).*

makes 2½ cups

3½ tablespoons chilled unsalted butter

4 shallots, roughly chopped

5 ounces button mushrooms or mushroom
   trimmings

1 bay leaf

a sprig of thyme

1¼ pounds white fish bones (sole, monkfish, or
   halibut), chopped

1¾ cups full-bodied red wine (Barolo is
   particularly good)

⅓ cup port

1 cup chicken or veal stock (see page 9)

3 tablespoons heavy cream

PG tip Some chefs finish the sauce, as I occasionally do, by turning the remaining butter into a noisette butter (see page 35), which is whisked into the sauce after the cream. I find it gives the sauce a more rounded flavor, but either way is equally delicious.

1 Heat 2 tablespoons of the butter in a large, heavy pan, then add the shallots, mushrooms, bay leaf, and thyme. Cook for 4–5 minutes until the vegetables are lightly golden.

2 Place the fish bones on top of the vegetables, cover, and cook for 2–3 minutes.

3 Add the wine and simmer, uncovered, for 5 minutes.

4 Add the port and stock and bring to a boil. Reduce the heat and simmer gently for another 25 minutes.

5 Strain through a fine mesh strainer into another pan and bring to a boil.

6 Add the cream and the remaining butter, cut into small pieces, and whisk until smooth.

Variations

CILANTRO RED WINE JUS

A wonderful sauce to accompany meaty fish such as sea bass, halibut, or turbot. At the end, simply add 2 tablespoons chopped cilantro and cook it in the sauce for 1 minute to infuse the flavors.

Alternatively, replace the cilantro with another herb of your choice—tarragon and flat-leaf parsley are particularly good.

ANCHOVY FISH JUS

The anchovy flavor makes this a lovely accompaniment for sole or turbot. Add 1 teaspoon anchovy paste to the finished sauce.

GRAIN MUSTARD AND BALSAMIC JUS

Add 2 teaspoons balsamic vinegar and 1 teaspoon Pommery grain mustard to the sauce at the end of cooking. Wonderful with white fish, roasted or grilled.

VEGETARIAN JUS

This sauce has opened up many new possibilities for the vegetarian cook and has really evolved only with the rise in popularity of vegetarian cuisine over the last 10–15 years. Optimal caramelizing of the vegetables is vital to bring out the natural flavors, and at the same time to enrich the color and appearance of the sauce.

makes 4 cups

2 tablespoons vegetable oil

4 shallots, chopped

5 ounces carrots, roughly chopped

2 ounces celery, roughly chopped

2 garlic cloves, crushed

a pinch of sugar

7 ounces mushrooms or mushrooms trimmings, chopped

4 ripe tomatoes, chopped

1 tablespoon tomato paste or passata

2 sprigs of thyme

6 cups dark vegetable stock (see page 10)

1/3 cup Madeira

3 tablespoons port

1 tablespoon light soy sauce

3 tablespoons arrowroot, mixed with a little water

1 Heat the oil in a large pan and add the shallots, carrots, celery, garlic, and sugar. Fry over medium-high heat until the vegetables are golden, about 15 minutes.

2 Add the mushrooms and fry for 3–4 minutes until golden. Add the tomatoes, tomato paste, and thyme, and cook, covered, for 5 minutes.

3 Add the stock and bring to a boil. Skim off any impurities and simmer for 15 minutes.

4 Add the Madeira, port, and soy sauce, and simmer for another 30 minutes.

5 Add the arrowroot, to thicken the sauce slightly, then strain through a fine mesh strainer.

Variations

WILD MUSHROOM AND TRUFFLE JUS

For a richer mushroomy sauce, replace the mushrooms with 2/3 ounce dried wild mushrooms, soaked in water for 20 minutes, then proceed as for the basic recipe. At the end, finish the strained sauce by whisking in 2 teaspoons truffle oil and 2 teaspoons butter.

LICORICE JUS

An unusual sauce which I love spooned over a creamy risotto of cauliflower or butternut squash. Add 2 tablespoons chopped chewy soft licorice along with the wines and soy sauce, then proceed as for the basic recipe.

BOUILLABAISSE-STYLE JUS

Created along the lines of the famous Provençale fish sauce or soup, this is particularly good served with green vegetables such as spinach, asparagus, leeks, or braised fennel. Replace the mushrooms with 2 chopped red peppers.

LENTIL AND TOMATO SAUCE

A rich, earthy-flavored sauce, wonderful with stuffed vegetables such as rice-filled eggplants. Add 3½ ounces soaked puy lentils (French lentils), 2 tablespoons balsamic vinegar, and 1 cup chopped tomatoes at the same time as the stock, then proceed as for the basic recipe.

TOMATO SAUCE

Tomatoes are world food; you will find them in almost every section of this book. This tomato sauce is a simple yet extremely effective and versatile sauce for any cook. Unlike its more rustic Sicilian cousin (see page 87), it has a smooth finish.

Do not be tempted to blitz the finished sauce in a blender or food processor, as the sauce can lose its wonderful rich red color. When your tomatoes are not as ripe or red as you would like, which can generally be the case except during the summer months, don't be afraid to replace them with good-quality canned varieties. In fact, most Italian chefs and cooks prefer to use these as good-quality canned often offer excellent flavor and color, something that fresh tomatoes cannot always do.

makes 4 cups

1 tablespoon unsalted butter

¼ cup olive oil

2 shallots (or 1 large onion), chopped

a sprig of thyme

1 small bay leaf

3 garlic cloves, crushed

2¼ pounds overripe vine plum tomatoes (preferably San Marzano), seeded and chopped (or 2 x 14½-ounce cans)

2 tablespoons tomato paste

1 tablespoon sugar

⅓ cup tomato juice (optional)

salt and freshly cracked black pepper

1 Put the butter and oil in a pan and add the shallots, thyme, bay leaf, and garlic. Sweat over a low heat until the shallots are softened and translucent.

2 Add the tomatoes, paste, sugar, and tomato juice, if using. Bring to a boil, then reduce the heat and simmer, uncovered, for 20–25 minutes.

3 Use a ladle to press the sauce through a fine mesh strainer. Season to taste.

Variation

ROASTED TOMATO SAUCE

Use only fresh tomatoes for this. Cut the tomatoes in half, rub each with a little of the garlic and place on a baking tray. Drizzle the olive oil over them and then sprinkle the thyme leaves on top. Season lightly with salt and pepper and roast in a preheated 250°F oven for 40 minutes, until the tomatoes are very soft. Add the roasted tomatoes to the recipe as in step 2 of the basic recipe, left, and proceed as described there.

RAW TOMATO SAUCE

For me, this can be made successfully only during the hot summer months when the vine-ripened tomatoes are succulent and sweet-tasting. A food mill or ricer-style strainer gives the best results, but a blender is also fine. ⊕ *This sauce is beautiful served with pasta, fish, and shellfish.*

makes 2 cups

1 pound overripe vine plum tomatoes (preferably San Marzano), chopped

1 tablespoon tomato paste

10 basil leaves

1 tablespoon sugar

2 tablespoons sherry, or raspberry, vinegar

⅓ cup olive oil

salt and freshly cracked black pepper

1 In a bowl, combine the tomatoes, tomato paste, basil, sugar, and vinegar. Cover and leave at room temperature for 2 hours.

2 Puree the mixture by putting it through a food mill (or blender) to form a smooth sauce.

3 Whisk in the oil, season to taste, and serve at room temperature. The sauce is best used quickly, while super-fresh tasting.

SAUCE AMÉRICAINE

⊕ *This shellfish sauce uses the carcass shells of lobster, shrimp, or crab, and results in a wonderful cream-based sauce for fish dishes.*

makes 4 cups

¾ stick unsalted butter

1 pound lobster, shrimp, or crab shells, broken up
   into small pieces

1 stalk of celery, finely chopped

1 carrot, finely chopped

1 onion, finely chopped

2 garlic cloves, crushed

⅓ cup brandy

½ cup all-purpose flour

⅔ cup dry white wine

6 large tomatoes, roughly chopped

3 tablespoons tomato paste

⅓ ounce tarragon leaves

4 cups fish (or chicken) stock (see pages 8 and 9)

8 white peppercorns, crushed

⅓ cup heavy cream

1 Heat the butter in a large, heavy pan and add the shells. Fry for 2–3 minutes.

2 Add the chopped vegetables and garlic, and cook for another 5 minutes. Add the brandy and cook for 1 minute.

3 Add the flour and make a roux around the shells and vegetables. Cook for 2–3 minutes, then add the wine and cook for another 2–3 minutes.

4 Stir in the tomatoes, tomato paste, tarragon, and stock, and bring to a boil, stirring.

5 Add the peppercorns and simmer for 40 minutes over a low heat, skimming off any impurities that rise to the surface.

6 In a separate pan, boil the cream, then stir it into the sauce. Strain through a fine mesh strainer.

VINAIGRETTES AND DRESSINGS

A cold, emulsified sauce, vinaigrette is also known as a salad dressing, and is one of the simplest of cold sauces to make. I always have a batch of classic vinaigrette in my fridge: it not only brings a salad to life, but also forms the base flavor.

For a good vinaigrette, I insist on two things: top-quality vinegar, such as white wine, champagne, sherry, red wine or balsamic, along with a mixture of a mild-tasting olive oil and a non-scented oil. In general, a ratio of three to four parts oil to one part vinegar will produce a very acceptable vinaigrette.

I include here my favorite classic vinaigrette recipe along with a few well-tested variations.

CLASSIC VINAIGRETTE

makes ⅔ cup

2 teaspoons Dijon mustard
2 tablespoons good-quality red wine vinegar (cabernet sauvignon)
salt and freshly cracked black pepper
¼ cup vegetable or sunflower oil
¼ cup mild olive oil

1 In a bowl, mix the mustard and vinegar with some salt and pepper.
2 Gradually add in the oils one at a time, in a thin stream, whisking constantly, until emulsified. Check the seasoning.

PG tip There are some interesting smoked olive oils entering the marketplace at the moment and I believe they will become more popular in future, so watch out for them. A smoked olive oil in classic vinaigrette will add an interesting smoky overtone to a salad.

Variations

GARLIC VINAIGRETTE

Add 1 finely crushed garlic clove to the bowl with the salt and pepper. Proceed as for the basic recipe, then let it stand for 1 hour before using to allow the flavors to infuse.

NUT OIL VINAIGRETTE

Use sherry vinegar instead of wine vinegar and replace the olive oil with hazelnut or walnut oil. Proceed as for the basic recipe. Fantastic on a salad of crispy greens with grilled goat cheese.

RAVIGOTE VINAIGRETTE

Add to the basic vinaigrette 1 tablespoon each of chopped roasted peppers, capers, gherkins, hard-boiled eggs, flat-leaf parsley, and shallots. Great with grilled fish, artichokes, asparagus, and smoked fish.

NIÇOISE VINAIGRETTE

Add to the basic vinaigrette the zest of ¼ lemon, 1 tablespoon each of chopped capers, black olives, and chopped basil, 2 finely chopped canned anchovy fillets and 2 seeded, chopped ripe tomatoes. Great with grilled leeks, asparagus, grilled fish and shellfish, or over baked feta or goat cheese.

ANISE VINAIGRETTE

Adds a wonderful hint of licorice to the dressing. Put 1 shallot, 1 crushed garlic clove, and 1 teaspoon green peppercorns in a blender and blitz with the basic vinaigrette until fine. Transfer to a bowl and add 1 teaspoon lemon zest, a pinch of ground anise, and 1 tablespoon Pernod. Leave it for 1 hour to infuse before using. Wonderful added to chopped salad greens to accompany scallops or duck breasts.

CITRUS VINAIGRETTE

Add the juice and zest of 1 lime or lemon to the basic vinaigrette, along with ½ teaspoon sugar.

HONEY MUSTARD VINAIGRETTE

In a pan, heat 1 tablespoon grainy mustard and
2 tablespoons honey. Add the warm mixture to the
basic vinaigrette.

HERB-INFUSED VINAIGRETTE

Add 1 teaspoon each of chopped chervil, tarragon,
chives, parsley, and mint to the basic vinaigrette; or
use just one of the herbs.

TOFU BALSAMIC VINAIGRETTE

Put 2 ounces silken tofu, 1 crushed garlic clove,
1 tablespoon chopped fresh cilantro, and ¼ cup
water in a blender and blitz until smooth. Add to the
basic vinaigrette made with good-quality balsamic
vinegar (aged, if possible).

CARAMELIZED SQUASH AND ICED GOAT CHEESE SALAD

It is important to use a firm cheese for this dish,
which means choosing an aged variety such as
crottin de Chavignol.

serves 4

1 tablespoon olive oil

2 teaspoons unsalted butter

1 butternut squash, peeled, seeded, and
cut into 1-inch pieces

6 strips of bacon, cut into pieces

a small handful of walnut halves

salt and freshly cracked black pepper

¼ cup honey mustard vinaigrette
(see above)

a good bunch of watercress, trimmed

1 firm goat cheese, about 3 ounces, frozen

1 Heat the oil and butter in a large frying pan and
when it is hot add the squash and fry until golden,
about 3–4 minutes.

2 Add the bacon and walnuts and toss together.
Continue cooking until the squash is just tender and
retaining its shape. Season with salt and pepper.

3 Add the vinaigrette and heat for 1 minute.

4 Transfer the squash to a plate and scatter the
watercress over it.

5 Remove the goat cheese from the freezer and
finely grate it over the salad. Serve immediately.

CREAMY VINAIGRETTES

Vinaigrettes are delicious when made into creamy-
style dressings, with the addition of a little light
cream, yogurt, mayonnaise, soft cheeses, or curd
cheese. Here are a few of my favorites:

ROQUEFORT DRESSING

Put ⅔ cup Roquefort (or another blue cheese of
your choice) in a blender with ⅓ cup light cream,
2 teaspoons sherry vinegar and ¼ cup olive oil. Add
2 tablespoons warm water and blitz until smooth.

WHITE SOFT CHEESE DRESSING

In a pan, gently heat 3 tablespoons cream almost
to a boil, then add 1 cup ripe Camembert, Brie, or
a soft goat cheese. Remove from the heat and
stir until melted. Set aside to cool, then add to the
basic vinaigrette.

WARM, COOKED SALAD DRESSINGS

Warm salad dressings are great during the summer months for those who enjoy light sauces with their food. They are particularly good with fish and shellfish as well as grilled poultry. They can be prepared in advance and reheated slowly.

SAUCE VIERGE

⊕ *A warm dressing for fish or shellfish, with provençale overtones.*

makes ⅔ cup

⅓ cup extra virgin olive oil

1 garlic clove, crushed

2 small canned anchovy fillets in oil, drained and finely diced (optional)

2 plum tomatoes, seeded and cut into small pieces

juice of ½ lemon

2 tablespoons chopped basil

1 tablespoon chopped flat-leaf parsley

salt and freshly cracked black pepper

1 Warm the oil and garlic in a small pan, then add the anchovies, if using, and tomatoes. Warm gently for 2 minutes to infuse the flavors and soften the tomatoes.

2 Stir in the lemon juice and herbs and season to taste.

Variations

SAUCE ANTIBOISE

Another provençale sauce, first discovered in the port of Antibes. Replace the basil and parsley in sauce vierge, left, with fresh cilantro leaves, and add ½ teaspoon toasted and lightly cracked coriander seeds to the warmed oil and garlic at the beginning of the recipe.

ORANGE AND GREEN PEPPERCORN SAUCE

Heat ¼ cup olive oil in a pan and add 1 chopped shallot and 1 crushed garlic clove. Cook until softened. Add ⅓ cup fresh or concentrated orange juice and whisk until amalgamated. Add 1 teaspoon green peppercorns and season to taste. Great poured over pan-fried fish, such as skate or cod.

EUROPE and the mediterranean

The sauces of this region encompass a wide variety of styles and flavorings, but they all share a sense of appropriateness to the climate and country to which they belong. The light, fragrant avgolémono of Greece, made with egg and lemon, is perfectly refreshing on a hot day; the robust, warming horseradish creams of Germany, served with smoked fish and meats, are ideally suited to a cold climate; while the fiery piri piri of Portugal and romescu of Spain are designed to cool you down in sweltering temperatures. In Italy you can even track the changes in climate and agriculture from north to south by the style of its regional sauces—from robust meat ragús or cream sauces in the cooler, dairy-loving north all the way down to the tomato- and olive-oil-based sauces of the arid south. The UK has perhaps the least clearly defined culinary profile of any European country, yet its sauces have a character all of their own: well-loved favorites such as bread sauce with poultry and mint sauce with lamb date back to medieval times and are a vital part of the culinary landscape.

SAVORY FRUIT SAUCES

Most of the traditional savory fruit sauces we still enjoy in Britain today, such as apple or gooseberry, date back to the 15th century. Research shows that in those days they tended to be sweeter and almost always spiced. Modern sauces have evolved into a more sweet-savory affair. The majority of fruit sauces are quick and uncomplicated preparations, the fruit cooked in a sweet syrup and simply served with roasted meats and game. The recipes below make enough for about eight servings.

PEAR SAUCE

⊕ *This is a medieval recipe I have used for years and is great with roast duck, or spread on toast for breakfast.*

makes 2½ cups

1 pound ripe but firm pears, peeled, cored, and cut
   into pieces (about 3–3½ cups)
1 teaspoon ground cinnamon
1 pared strip of lemon rind
2 tablespoons granulated sugar
5 tablespoons water

1 Put the pears, cinnamon, lemon rind, and sugar in a pan. Bring to a boil, lower the heat, and cook until the pears have softened.
2 Transfer to a blender and blitz to a puree. Serve warm or cold.

APPLESAUCE

Use tart Bramley cooking apples for best results.

makes 2½ cups

14 ounces apples, peeled, cored, and thickly sliced
⅓ cup water
2 tablespoons granulated sugar
juice of 1 lemon
2 tablespoons unsalted butter

1 Put the apple pieces in a pan with the water, sugar, and lemon juice, and bring to a boil.
2 Simmer for 10–12 minutes or until the apples have softened.
3 Let cool, then press it through a fine strainer, or puree in a blender.
4 Return to the heat, stir in the butter, and serve warm.

SPICY CRANBERRY SAUCE

⊕ *It's a terrible waste to save this tart fruit sauce for the Thanksgiving turkey, as it's also very good with duck, game, roast ham, and cold meats.*

makes 2½ cups

1 pound fresh or frozen cranberries (about 5 cups)
1 cup demerara sugar (raw sugar)
finely grated zest of 1 orange and juice of 2 oranges
½ teaspoon apple pie spice

1 Put all the ingredients in a pan and bring slowly to a boil, stirring until the sugar has dissolved. Lower the heat and simmer for 30 minutes until the berries are very soft. Serve warm or at room temperature.

QUINCE SAUCE

Quinces are not always easy to come by and take a long time to cook, but they are really worth the trouble. ⊕ *Great with game and especially roast pork.*

makes 2½ cups

14 ounces firm quinces, peeled

⅓ cup water

1 cup granulated sugar

1 teaspoon finely grated lemon zest

1 Using a very good, heavy knife, cut the quinces into pieces, discarding the cores, and put in a pan with the remaining ingredients.

2 Cook gently over a low heat for up to 1¼ hours, until dark amber in color. Puree in a blender.

GOOSEBERRY SAUCE

⊕ *A lovely, seasonal fruit sauce: tart in flavor and wonderful with oily fish and roast pork.*

makes 2½ cups

14 ounces fresh or frozen gooseberries (about 3½ cups)

⅓ cup water

½ cup granulated sugar

2 tablespoons unsalted butter

1 Put the gooseberries in a pan with the water and ¼ cup of the sugar and bring to a boil. Reduce the heat and simmer for 10–15 minutes, until softened.

2 Transfer to a blender and blitz to a puree, then add the remaining sugar.

3 Return to the pan to heat through. Stir in the butter and serve warm.

Variation

Add some freshly chopped mint leaves to the finished sauce.

CUMBERLAND SAUCE

Purists may be surprised to see a variation of this classic fruit sauce flavored with blueberry jam (see page 71), rather than red currant jelly. I tried it one Christmas served with beautifully sliced gammon when I didn't have any red currant jelly, and I found I actually preferred the blueberry version, as did my guests. ⊕ *Both versions are wonderful served with cold turkey, duck, or goose.*

makes 1¼ cups

grated zest and juice of 1 small orange

grated zest and juice of 1 lemon

9 ounces red currant jelly

1 teaspoon Dijon mustard

5 tablespoons port

½ teaspoon ground ginger

1 large shallot, finely chopped

salt and freshly cracked black pepper

1 Put the zest of the orange and lemon in a small saucepan of boiling water. Boil for 2 minutes, then drain and set aside.

2 Put the red currant jelly, mustard, and port into a pan and mix. Add the ginger and gently heat until the jam melts, but do not boil.

3 Add the orange and lemon juice, the drained zest, and the shallot. Season to taste and serve at room temperature.

Cumberland sauce
variation

BLUEBERRY
CUMBERLAND SAUCE
Replace the red currant jelly
with 9 ounces blueberry jam
(about 1 cup).

OLD-FASHIONED BREAD SAUCE

⊕ *Roasted game and fowl in season would not be complete without this creamy and delicately spiced bread sauce.* The addition of a little heavy cream and butter enriches it beautifully.

makes 2½ cups

1 onion, cut in half

4 cloves

2 cups whole milk

¼ cup heavy cream

1⅓ cups fresh white breadcrumbs

2 tablespoons chilled unsalted butter, cut into small pieces

salt and freshly cracked black pepper

freshly grated nutmeg

1 Stud the onion halves with the cloves and put in a pan with the milk and half of the cream. Bring gently to a boil, then remove from the heat and let it infuse for 10 minutes.

2 Strain the milk into a clean pan and reheat almost to boiling point, then whisk in the breadcrumbs and cook for 2 minutes, until the sauce thickens.

3 Add the remaining cream and stir in the chilled butter pieces.

4 Season with salt, pepper, and nutmeg, to taste.

PG tip Bread sauce must be made when needed, kept warm, and served immediately, as it doesn't take kindly to reheating.

MINT SAUCE

⊕ *Traditionally served with roast or grilled lamb, mint sauce, with its pungent piquant flavor, is the perfect foil for the rich, fatty-tasting meat.*

makes ⅔ cup

3½ ounces mint leaves (about 6–7 handfuls)

2 tablespoons sugar

2 tablespoons malt vinegar, or to taste

1 Using a mortar and pestle, crush the mint leaves and sugar to a coarse pulp. Set aside for 30 minutes to allow the sugar to draw the juices from the mint.

2 Stir in the vinegar, to taste.

Variation

BALSAMIC MINT SAUCE

Replace the malt vinegar with sweet-tasting balsamic vinegar.

GERMAN HORSERADISH SAUCE

In Britain we prefer our horseradish sauce mixed with cream—to accompany one of our natural treasures, roast beef—but it can be omitted to create a sharper, or German, version. Always use fresh, crisp horseradish, as it loses its strong flavor the older it gets. ⊕ *Delicious with smoked fish.*

makes ¾–1 cup

1 fresh horseradish root, about 12 ounces
juice of ½ lemon
a good pinch of sugar
a pinch of salt
⅔ cup semi-whipped cream (optional)

1 Peel the horseradish and grate it finely into a bowl. Take care as the fumes can be extremely strong.
2 Add the lemon juice, sugar, and salt, to taste.
3 Stir in the semi-whipped cream, if using. Cover with plastic wrap and refrigerate until ready to use.

Variation

CHRAIN

Chrain is a sauce synonymous with Jewish cooking, traditionally served with smoked fish. Add 2 tablespoons plain yogurt and 2 finely grated raw beets to the basic sauce.

PG tip A good way to protect your face from the eye-watering pungency of horseradish is to cover your nose with a paint mask.

SMOKED EEL WITH POTATO, ASPARAGUS, AND HORSERADISH VINAIGRETTE

serves 4

12 asparagus spears, trimmed
8 quail eggs
1 ounce arugula leaves (about ½ cup)
1 ounce curly chicory (about ¾ cup)
½ ounce chervil sprigs
4 skinless smoked eel fillets, 10 ounces each, cut into 2-inch lengths
1 sweet dill pickle, sliced
10 ounces cooked new potatoes, thinly sliced

for the horseradish vinaigrette

½ teaspoon horseradish sauce (see left)
5 tablespoons olive oil
1 tablespoon chopped flat-leaf parsley
1 teaspoon white wine vinegar

1 Make the vinaigrette by placing all the ingredients in a bowl and whisking until amalgamated.
2 Cook the asparagus in boiling, salted water for 2 minutes, then remove to ice water to refresh. Drain and dry.
3 Hard-boil the quail eggs for 3 minutes, then remove to ice water. Peel and cut each in half.
4 Toss the arugula, chicory, and chervil together in a bowl, then divide between 4 serving plates.
5 Place the eel fillets on the salad greens, with the egg halves and sliced pickle.
6 Put the potatoes and asparagus tips in a bowl, pour in a little horseradish vinaigrette, and toss to coat. Scatter them over the salad, drizzle any remaining dressing on top, and serve.

TAPENADE

One of the classic French provençale sauces, tapenade takes its name from the dialect word *tapeno*, meaning caper, which may seem a little strange given that the dominant ingredient of the dish is the wonderful niçoise black olive, so synonymous with the area. Tapenade can be kept in a sealed jar in the fridge for up to 3–4 months.

makes 1¼ cups

1 cup good-quality pitted black olives
6 canned anchovy fillets in oil, drained
⅓ cup capers, drained and rinsed
3 garlic cloves, crushed
⅔ cup olive oil
freshly cracked black pepper

1 Put the olives, anchovies, capers, and garlic in a blender and pulse 3–4 times, until coarsely chopped.
2 Using the feeder tube, with the motor running, add the oil in a thin stream.
3 Transfer to a bowl and add some black pepper.

Variation

TOMATO TAPENADE

Replace the olives with semi-dried tomatoes and 1 teaspoon each of thyme leaves and chopped rosemary. Proceed as for the main recipe.

PG tip Use either version of the tapenade as a pungent sauce to enliven sandwiches, goat cheese, grilled meats or fish.

PROVENÇALE TOASTS WITH SEA BASS AND TAPENADE

serves 4

4 slices of good-quality country-style bread, about an inch thick, or 8 slices of baguette, cut diagonally, about ¾-inch thick
¼ cup extra virgin olive oil
4 small fillets of sea bass, about 4 ounces each, cleaned
salt and freshly cracked black pepper
2 garlic cloves
2 tablespoons chopped herbes de Provence (basil, chervil, rosemary, and parsley)
⅓ cup tapenade (see left)

1 Heat a grill pan over a high heat. Brush both sides of the bread with olive oil.
2 Grill the bread until lightly charred, about 1 minute per side. Remove and keep warm. Meanwhile, season the sea bass liberally with salt and pepper.
3 Add the fish to the grill pan and cook for 2–3 minutes on each side.
4 Rub the hot grilled toasts with the garlic and a little more oil, and sprinkle with the herbs.
5 Place a grilled piece of sea bass on each piece of toast (cut each piece of fish in half if you are using the smaller slices of baguette). Top with a spoonful of tapenade and serve immediately.

PESTO

As a bit of a traditionalist, I make my pesto by using a mortar and pestle to pound the ingredients before adding the oil, but in this modern world a blender does a quicker and equally successful job. It will keep in the fridge for 2–3 days before losing its vibrant color and freshness.

makes about ⅔ cup

2½ ounces basil leaves
2 garlic cloves, chopped
1 tablespoon roughly chopped pine nuts
2 tablespoons finely grated Parmesan cheese
    (preferably Reggiano)
⅓ cup extra virgin olive oil
salt and freshly cracked black pepper

1 Put the basil, garlic, pine nuts, and Parmesan in a blender. With the motor running, slowly pour in the oil in a thin stream through the feeder tube, and blend until smooth.
2 Add salt and pepper to taste, transfer to a bowl (or container with a lid), cover and refrigerate until needed.

PG tip You can replace the basil with another favorite herb: flat-leaf parsley, cilantro, or mint, for example. Or try one of the variations on this page.

Variations

PUMPKIN SEED AND GOAT CHEESE PESTO

Replace the pine nuts with 1¾ cups pumpkin seeds, baked in a moderate oven (375°F) for 10 minutes until lightly golden and fragrant, then cooled. Replace the basil with 1¾ ounces mint (about 3 cups), and use 3 tablespoons soft goat cheese instead of the Parmesan. Proceed as for the basic recipe.

ASPARAGUS PESTO

Trim and remove the woody ends of 8 asparagus spears and cook in boiling, salted water for 2 minutes. Refresh in ice water to stop them cooking further, then dry them well with a cloth. Cut the asparagus into small pieces and add to the blender along with the other ingredients in the main recipe. Serve with either pasta or grilled fish.

ARUGULA PESTO

Replace the basil with arugula leaves for a hotter pesto.

RAPINI PESTO (BROCCOLI RAAB)

This pesto is served warm, tossed with pasta. Cook 5½ ounces broccoli spears in boiling water, until very soft. Drain well, put in a blender, and blitz until coarsely pureed. Add all the ingredients from the main recipe and blitz again for 10 seconds.

HAZELNUT PESTO

Replace the pine nuts with 3 tablespoons chopped hazelnuts. Omit the Parmesan and add ½ teaspoon red pepper flakes instead.

TROFIE TRAPENESE STYLE

This is a Sicilian pasta dish that blends tomatoes into the pesto, and uses local almonds instead of pine nuts.

serves 4

⅓ cup whole almonds

2 garlic cloves, crushed

1 small red chile with seeds, finely chopped

salt and freshly cracked black pepper

⅔ ounce mint leaves, preferably spearmint

1¾ ounces basil leaves

1 ounce Romano cheese (or Parmigiano-Reggiano)

⅓ cup extra virgin olive oil

3 large, ripe but firm tomatoes, peeled and cut into small pieces

1 pound trofie pasta (or bucatini or spirals)

1 Put the almonds, garlic, chile, and a little salt and pepper in a blender. Blitz until everything is very roughly chopped.

2 Add the mint, basil, cheese, and oil, and blitz again until the herbs are chopped and the mixture is blended. The texture should be chunky, not pureed.

3 Transfer to a bowl, toss in the tomatoes, and add salt and pepper, to taste.

4 Cook the pasta in a large pot of boiling, salted water, until just cooked, or *al dente*.

5 Drain the pasta, toss with the sauce, and serve immediately.

FONDUTA

Often confused with the classic Swiss fondue, fonduta is a similar sauce from Italy's Piedmont region. Fontina is the cheese of choice, although it can successfully be made with other cheeses, such as Gruyère, Emmenthal, or even Dutch Edam —anything rich and creamy. ⊕ *For a real treat, scatter some freshly shaved white truffles over the top. One of the nicest dishes I have ever tasted in Italy was in Sicily where fonduta was served over some simple poached eggs, with the shaved white truffle on top—highly recommended!*

makes 2½ cups

12 ounces fontina cheese, cut into small cubes

1 teaspoon cornstarch

2½ cups whole milk

salt and freshly cracked black pepper

4 cage-free eggs, beaten

¾ stick unsalted butter, cut into small cubes

1 Put the cheese, cornstarch, and milk in a small pan with a little salt and pepper. Place over a low heat, stirring constantly, until the cheese has melted. It will become a little stringy.

2 Beat the eggs and butter in vigorously and continue cooking over a low heat until the sauce becomes runny, creamy, and smooth.

3 Pour into bowls or ramekins and serve immediately with chunks of crusty bread.

Variation

Add 2 tablespoons grappa to the finished fonduta: lovely with chicken.

SALSA VERDE

(Italian green sauce)

Salsa verde is a rustic sauce, served cold, and is different all over Italy. Some versions include bread soaked in vinegar, some have chopped egg—the variations are endless. ⊕ *Used as a condiment for meat, fish, poultry, and vegetable dishes, for me it's the greatest sauce in Italian cooking.*

makes 1¼ cups

1 garlic clove

1 ounce flat-leaf parsley, leaves only, roughly chopped

⅔ cup mint leaves, roughly chopped

4 canned anchovy fillets in oil, drained

1 teaspoon Dijon mustard

⅔ ounce sweet dill-pickled gherkins

⅓ cup superfine capers in brine, drained and rinsed

2 tablespoons white wine vinegar

½ cup extra virgin olive oil

salt and freshly cracked black pepper

1 Crush the garlic with a mortar and pestle, then add the herbs and anchovy fillets. Crush to a pulp.

2 Add the mustard, gherkins, and capers, then crush to a puree-like consistency.

3 Add the vinegar, then slowly drizzle in the olive oil to form a semi-fluid sauce. Season to taste, and serve. Salsa verde will keep in a sealed container in the fridge for 2–3 days.

ROAST PORK BELLY WITH BLACK CABBAGE AND SALSA VERDE

⊕ *Delicious with mashed potatoes finished with olive oil rather than butter.*

serves 4

2¼-pound piece of boneless pork belly

salt and freshly cracked black pepper

2 teaspoons fennel seeds

¼ cup olive oil

1¾ cups dry white wine

2½ cups veal or chicken stock (see pages 8 and 9)

1 large cavolo nero (Tuscan Kale) or savoy cabbage, about 1¼ pounds

1 onion, finely chopped

1 garlic clove, crushed

⅓ cup water

⅔ cup salsa verde (see left), for serving

1 Preheat the oven to 425°F. Cut the pork into 4 equal-sized slabs and rub with salt, pepper, and fennel seeds. Place in a shallow roasting pan, drizzle half the oil over it, and put into the oven for 20–25 minutes, to start off the crackling.

2 Remove the pork from the oven and reduce the heat to 350°F. Pour the wine and stock around the pork. Return to the oven to cook for another 1–1¼ hours, or until the pork is very tender.

3 Meanwhile, pull the cabbage leaves from the base of the stalk and shred them coarsely. Heat the remaining oil in a pan, add the onion and garlic, and cook for 3–4 minutes, then add the cabbage and water. Cover, lower the heat, and cook gently for 30–40 minutes.

4 When the pork is cooked, remove from the oven and strain any juices remaining in the pan into a small pan. Boil to reduce the juices to about 1 tablespoon, or until they coat the back of a spoon.

5 To serve, put the pork pieces onto serving plates (on mashed potato, ideally) with the reduced juices drizzled over them. Add the cabbage to each serving. Spoon the salsa verde on top and serve.

CARBONARA SAUCE

One of the great Italian sauces, rich and extremely
unctuous in flavor, carbonara does not traditionally
contain any cream. Many cooks, however, feel that
the addition of a little cream helps to stabilize the
sauce. Although it is generally felt Parmesan is the
preferred cheese, any Italian will tell you nothing
other than Romano will do!

serves 4

2 tablespoons olive oil

¼ pound salt pork or smoked bacon, cut into very
    small pieces

1 garlic clove, crushed

3 cage-free eggs, lightly beaten

2 tablespoons heavy cream (optional)

1 pound dried pasta

2 ounces Romano (or Parmigiano-Reggiano)
    cheese, finely grated

salt and freshly cracked black pepper

1 Heat the oil in a pan, add the pork or bacon, and
cook until golden all over. Add the garlic and cook
for 1 minute.
2 In a bowl, mix the eggs with the cream, if using.
3 Meanwhile, cook the pasta until just done, or
al dente. Drain well, then add to the bacon and
garlic pan. Pour the eggs, or eggs and cream over
the pasta, quickly add the Romano, and toss to mix.
Add salt and pepper to taste and serve immediately.

Variation

FUNGHI CARBONARA

Replace the bacon with 5 ounces fresh, wild
mushrooms (or ½ ounce dried and soaked).
Proceed as for the main recipe.

PG tip Carbonara is also
excellent stirred into scrambled
eggs and served on thick,
crisp toast.

RAGÙ BOLOGNESE

Although I have not included many sauces that
contain meat or fish, I felt I had to include this one,
because it is so popular. Bolognese sauce as a
name doesn't actually exist in Italy, where it is just
called a ragù sauce. Tradition has it that the longer
the sauce cooks, the better the flavor.

serves 4–6, with pasta

3½ tablespoons unsalted butter

½ cup pancetta or smoked bacon, cut into
    small pieces

1 onion, finely chopped

1 carrot, finely chopped

1 stalk of celery, finely chopped

2 teaspoons chopped oregano

2 teaspoons thyme leaves

1½ cups good-quality lean ground beef

3½ ounces chicken livers, cleaned well
    and chopped

2 tablespoons tomato paste

⅓ cup dry white wine

1¼ cups beef stock (see page 9)

salt and freshly cracked black pepper

freshly grated nutmeg

1 Melt the butter in a large, heavy pan, add the
pancetta, and fry for 4–5 minutes, or until golden.
2 Add the onion, carrot, celery, and herbs, and cook
for another 2 minutes.
3 Stir in the ground beef, increase the heat, and
brown the meat well all over.
4 Add the chopped livers and cook for 2 minutes.
Stir in the tomato paste and cook for 5 minutes.
5 Add the wine and stock, then season lightly with
salt, pepper, and nutmeg.
6 Bring to a boil, reduce to a low simmer and cook,
covered, for at least 30 minutes.

RAGÙ BOLOGNESE
Classically served with
Italian noodles, it is
also great spooned
over fresh gnocchi.

ALMOND AND CAPER SALSA

I first tasted this sauce while on vacation on the beautiful island of Sardinia, at a small restaurant on the Cala di Volpe. It formed a sort of dressing for an eggplant salad, and was wonderful. I have recreated the combination here.

In essence, it is similar to pesto in texture but with added acidic qualities from the capers—a balance of flavors that really works.

makes 1 cup

½ cup blanched almonds, lightly toasted

2½ tablespoons superfine capers, drained and rinsed

a pinch of dried red pepper flakes

⅓ cup extra virgin olive oil

1 garlic clove, crushed

1 ounce mint leaves (about 1½–2 cups)

juice of 1 small lemon

salt

1 Put the almonds, capers, and red pepper flakes in a blender and blitz to a coarse purée.

2 Heat the oil with the garlic in a pan until warm, then add the mint. Cook for 30 seconds over a very low heat, just to let the flavors infuse.

3 Remove from the heat and let cool, then add, through the feeder tube and with the motor running, to the almond and olive mixture in the blender.

4 Add the lemon juice, and salt to taste, then transfer the salsa to a bowl and let cool completely before serving.

ROASTED EGGPLANT AND TOMATO SALAD WITH ALMOND AND CAPER SALSA

serves 4

2 large eggplants, cut into 1-inch cubes

2 tablespoons olive oil

1 garlic clove, sliced

2 ripe, firm tomatoes, chopped

1 small onion, chopped

2 tablespoons red wine vinegar

salt and freshly cracked black pepper

2 tablespoons small mint leaves, for garnishing

3 tablespoons almond and caper salsa (see left)

1 Preheat the oven to 350°F. Place the eggplant cubes in a large roasting pan, drizzle the oil over them, and toss to coat.

2 Add the garlic, toss again, then roast in the oven until tender, about 20–25 minutes. Turn the eggplant cubes occasionally as they cook.

3 Transfer to a bowl and let cool. Add the tomatoes, onion, and vinegar, and season to taste.

4 Scatter the top with the mint leaves and serve with the almond and caper salsa.

PG tip

In some parts of Italy they like to roast the garlic for this recipe, giving the sauce a sweeter, more caramelized flavor.

AGLIATA

An Italian sauce made from pounded walnuts,
particularly good with pasta and fish.

makes ¾–1 cup

2 slices of stale white bread, crusts removed
¼ cup chicken stock (see page 9)
1 tablespoon balsamic or red wine vinegar
1 cup walnut halves, lightly toasted
1¾ ounces flat-leaf parsley, leaves only
2 garlic cloves, crushed
salt and freshly cracked black pepper
⅓ cup extra virgin olive oil

1 Soak the bread in the stock for 2–3 minutes, then
squeeze out the excess moisture, using your hands.
2 Put the bread in a blender along with the vinegar,
walnuts, parsley, garlic, and some salt and pepper.
3 Using the feeder tube and with the motor
running, slowly pour in the olive oil until you have a
thickish paste-like sauce.
4 Adjust the seasoning and serve. Agliata will keep,
covered, in the fridge for 1 day.

LINGUINE WITH RED MULLET
AND AGLIATA (for 4 people)

Season with salt and pepper 1 pound small,
cleaned red mullet (or red snapper) fillets and
fry in a mixture of olive oil and unsalted butter for
1 minute on each side. Squeeze some lemon juice
over them. Meanwhile, cook 1 pound linguine in
boiling, salted water until cooked, then drain and
toss with ¾–1 cup agliata sauce. Serve with the
fried mullet pieces.

SALMORIGLIO

What I adore about this Sicilian garlic, lemon, and herb-oil sauce is the way so few ingredients can make something taste so good with fish. I have adapted this recipe from one I tasted on the beautiful island of Sicily. ⊕ *Drizzle it over char-grilled fish and poultry, or use it as a marinade for fish or shellfish.*

makes ⅔ cup

⅓ cup extra virgin olive oil (preferably Sicilian)
1 garlic clove, crushed
2 tablespoons warm water
2 tablespoons chopped oregano
1 tablespoon chopped flat-leaf parsley
juice of ½ lemon
salt and freshly cracked black pepper

1 Whisk the olive oil and garlic together in a bowl, then add the water and whisk to form a light emulsion.
2 Add the herbs and lemon juice, and season to taste.

CHAR-GRILLED MONKFISH (ANGLER FISH) WITH CHICKPEAS, CHARD, AND SALMORIGLIO

serves 4

2 tablespoons olive oil
½ garlic clove, chopped
2 shallots, finely chopped
a pinch of dried red pepper flakes
1 cup canned tomatoes
1 tablespoon tomato paste
a pinch of sugar
1 small bay leaf
salt and freshly cracked black pepper
3 cups cooked dried chickpeas (or canned)
5 ounces Swiss chard leaves, shredded
1½ pounds cleaned monkfish (angler fish) fillet, cut into 4 thick pieces
⅔ cup salmoriglio (see left)

1 Heat 1 tablespoon of the oil in a heavy pan over medium heat. Add the garlic, shallots, and red pepper flakes and cook for 4–5 minutes, without browning.
2 Add the tomatoes, tomato paste, sugar, and bay leaf. Season, then bring to a boil and simmer for 10 minutes.
3 Add the chickpeas and chard, mix well, and cook over a low heat for another 5 minutes.
4 Meanwhile, heat a barbecue or grill pan until very hot. Season the monkfish pieces liberally with salt and pepper and drizzle the remaining oil over them.
5 Place the monkfish on the barbecue or grill pan and cook for 4 minutes on each side, until golden and lightly charred.
6 Put the chickpeas on a serving dish, top with the monkfish, drizzle the salmoriglio sauce over them, and serve.

SICILIAN TOMATO SAUCE

This rustic tomato sauce forms the base of many dishes in Italian cuisine, from pizza to pasta dishes. Ideally, use San Marzano tomatoes for this sauce, as they have a wonderful, sweet flavor. If your tomatoes are not well-flavored or of a good color, use canned.

makes 4 cups

2¼ pounds flavorful, ripe tomatoes or
    2 x 14½-ounce cans plum tomatoes
¼ cup olive oil
1 large onion, finely chopped
2 garlic cloves, crushed
1 tablespoon tomato paste
⅔ cup tomato juice
a pinch of sugar
½ teaspoon dried oregano
¼ teaspoon thyme leaves
salt and freshly cracked black pepper

1 If using fresh tomatoes, blanch them in boiling water for 20 seconds, then remove them with a slotted spoon directly into ice water. Peel and cut in half, then seed and chop finely.
2 Heat the oil in a heavy pan, add the onion and garlic, and cook until soft, about 10 minutes.
3 Add the chopped tomatoes and tomato paste and cook for 5 minutes.
4 Add the tomato juice, sugar, and herbs, and simmer, uncovered, for 1 hour over a low heat, until reduced to a pulpy consistency. Season to taste.

Variations
ARRABIATA SAUCE
Add 2 teaspoons chopped red chile to the onion and garlic at the beginning of the recipe.

AMATRICIANA SAUCE
Cook ¾ cup chopped pancetta or bacon in the oil until golden, before adding the onion and garlic.

PIRI PIRI

The burning question: is piri piri a sauce or a condiment? In Brazil it brightens up every dish, it seems, so this sauce also has a rightful place in the New World section of this book. However, in Portugal, where I am sure many people first taste it and where it accompanies countless chicken and fish dishes, it is every bit as ubiquitous and popular.

Piri piri sauce, so called after the chile of the same name, is enjoyed in lots of Mediterranean countries served right from a bottle: perfectly acceptable, you may say, but in no shape or form a match for the freshly made, preservative-free version here. It will keep for up to a month in the fridge.

makes 1½ cups

8 large red piri piri or jalapeño chiles
⅓ cup olive oil
1 cup tomato passata
1 teaspoon oregano
juice of 1 lemon
a pinch of chili powder
salt and freshly cracked black pepper

1 Put the chiles and oil in a blender and blitz to a smooth paste.
2 Transfer to a pan and add the passata, oregano, and lemon juice. Bring to a boil, then simmer for 10–15 minutes.
3 Add the chilli powder along with salt and pepper to taste.

ROMESCU

One of the great Spanish sauces, dating back hundreds of years to Tarragona in the Catalonia region. Whether made with hazelnuts or almonds, it never fails to impress. ⊕ *I think I've served it with just about every type of grilled fish, vegetable, meat, even fried eggs—utterly versatile.*

makes 1½ cups

⅔ cup extra virgin olive oil

1 slice of white bread, cut into cubes

3 garlic cloves, crushed

½ cup almonds or hazelnuts, lightly toasted

1 teaspoon dried red pepper flakes (or 1 dried red chile)

1 teaspoon smoked Spanish paprika

12 ounces roasted red peppers

3 tablespoons white wine vinegar

8 ounces tomatoes, blanched, peeled, seeded and chopped (see Sicilian tomato sauce, page 87, step 1)

salt and freshly cracked black pepper

1 Heat 2 tablespoons of the oil in a large frying pan, add the bread cubes, and fry until golden. Add the garlic, almonds or hazelnuts, red pepper flakes, and paprika, and cook for another 30 seconds.

2 Transfer to a blender and add the roasted peppers and vinegar. Blitz to a pulp. Using the feeder tube and with the motor running, gradually trickle in the remaining olive oil.

3 Add the tomatoes, blitz again, and season to taste.

Variation

SPICY ROMESCU VINAGRETTE

Add 2 tablespoons of the romescu sauce to ⅔ cup classic vinaigrette (see page 62). Great with grilled tuna or swordfish.

ROASTED SWORDFISH WITH FENNEL, PINE NUTS, AND RAISINS

serves 4

5 tablespoons olive oil

1 onion, thinly sliced

1 head of fennel, thinly sliced, fronds reserved and chopped

a pinch of sugar

⅓ cup pine nuts, lightly toasted

⅓ cup raisins, soaked in water for 20 minutes and drained

4 swordfish steaks, 7 ounces each

salt and freshly cracked black pepper

2 tablespoons chopped mint leaves

⅓ cup romescu sauce (see left)

1 Heat 3 tablespoons of the oil in a pan, add the onion, fennel, and sugar, and cook over a low heat until lightly caramelized and golden.

2 Add the pine nuts and drained raisins and cook for another 5 minutes.

3 Meanwhile, heat the remaining oil in a frying pan and season the fish. When the oil is hot, add the fish and cook for 1–2 minutes on each side until golden. Put the swordfish and fennel mixture on a plate.

4 Add the chopped mint and fennel fronds to the romescu sauce and serve alongside the swordfish.

AVGOLEMONO

One of the most popular and ubiquitous sauces in Greece, this lemon sauce is delicious served with meat and vegetables such as artichokes, leeks, or asparagus. ● *I particularly like it with foil-baked cod steaks on a melée of butter beans, tomato, and parsley, as in the recipe on the right.*

makes 1¾ cups

3 large cage-free egg yolks

juice of 2 lemons

2 teaspoons cornstarch

1 tablespoon water

1¼ cups well-flavored hot chicken stock
   (see page 8)

2 tablespoons sour cream

salt and freshly cracked black pepper

1 Whisk the egg yolks and lemon juice together in a heavy pan, off the heat.

2 Put the cornstarch and water in a jar with a lid and shake until dissolved. Stir it into the egg yolks in the pan.

3 Whisk the hot stock gradually into the eggs, a little at a time, until amalgamated, whisking constantly, then add the sour cream.

4 Place the pan over a low heat and cook, whisking continuously, until the mixture thickens enough to coat the back of a spoon. Make sure that it does not boil, or the sauce will curdle.

5 Season to taste and serve immediately.

PG tip Avgolemono is also the name of a soup made in Greece, of chicken broth with rice, finished with egg and lemon.

BAKED COD STEAKS WITH BUTTER BEANS AND AVGOLEMONO

You can substitute halibut for the cod, if you like.

serves 4

1 small onion, chopped

2 strips of bacon, chopped

1 tablespoon olive oil

1 garlic clove, crushed

¼ teaspoon dried red pepper flakes

½ cup dried butter beans (or dried limas)

3¼ cups well-flavored hot chicken stock
   (see page 8)

3 plum tomatoes, roughly chopped

1 tablespoon chopped flat-leaf parsley

salt and freshly cracked black pepper

4 cod steaks, 8 ounces each

2 shallots, thinly sliced

juice of ½ lemon

⅔ cup fish stock (see page 9)

⅔ cup avgolemono (see left), for serving

1 Preheat the oven to 325°F. In a large ovenproof and flameproof pan, sweat the onion and bacon in the oil over a low heat for 3–4 minutes. Add the garlic, red pepper flakes, and butter beans, and cook for 1 minute.

2 Pour in the chicken stock, bring to a boil, cover, and cook for 2 hours until the beans are very tender, adding a little extra stock or water if needed.

3 Stir in the tomatoes and parsley, season to taste, and remove from the heat.

4 Increase the oven temperature to 425°F. Place the fish steaks in a baking pan and scatter with the shallots. Add the lemon juice and fish stock, then season. Cover with foil and cook in the oven for 10–12 minutes, or until the fish is cooked through.

5 Divide the beans between 4 individual plates, top each with a baked cod steak, pour the hot avgolemono sauce over them, and serve immediately.

SKORDALIA

Skordalia (or as it is known throughout Greece, Skorthalia) is a delightful sauce of just four components: potatoes, olive oil, garlic, and lemon juice—magically simple. It works better when the potatoes are still warm, so don't let them go cold. In certain parts of Greece, chopped walnuts are added to the potatoes before blending. ⊕ *A great sauce for almost any fish, especially deep-fried. It also makes a useful dip at parties for vegetables or pita bread.*

makes about 3 cups

11 ounces floury potatoes, cut into chunks

4 garlic cloves, crushed

about ¾ cup extra virgin olive oil

juice of ½ large lemon

salt and freshly cracked black pepper

1 Put the potato chunks in a pan of cold water, bring to a boil, and simmer for 20–25 minutes until very soft. Drain well, then transfer to a food processor or blender.

2 Add the garlic and blitz quickly. With the motor running on its slowest possible setting, pour in enough oil in a thin stream to form an emulsion.

3 Add the lemon juice and enough warm water to achieve a mayonnaise-like consistency.

4 Season to taste, and serve.

Variation

Add ⅔ cup feta cheese to the hot potatoes in the blender, then proceed as for the main recipe.

PG tip Don't work the potatoes too long in the blender or food processor, as they will turn starchy and glutinous.

ROASTED BEETS WITH ARUGULA, SOFT EGG, AND SKORDALIA

serves 4

24 baby raw beets (or 2–3 larger beets, sliced)

2 tablespoons olive oil

salt and freshly cracked black pepper

4 cage-free eggs

1½ cups skordalia (see left)

3½ ounces baby arugula leaves

1 ounce cilantro leaves (optional)

2 tablespoons classic vinaigrette (see page 62)

1 Preheat the oven to 400°F. Trim the beets, leaving about an inch of long top attached. Trim the bottoms to remove any root.

2 Toss the beets in the olive oil and season with a little salt. Put them in a baking dish, cover with foil, and cook in the oven for up to 45 minutes, or until tender when pierced with a knife.

3 Remove from the oven and leave them until cool enough to handle, then peel. Season with salt and pepper and keep warm.

4 Cook the eggs in simmering water for 5 minutes so that the yolks are still soft in the middle. Remove, cool, and peel.

5 To serve, place some skordalia on the base of 4 serving plates, with the beets on top. Scatter the arugula (and cilantro if using) over them and drizzle the vinaigrette. Cut the eggs in half and add to each plate, then serve immediately.

TARATOR

This sauce is one of Turkey's greatest treasures. It is traditionally made with hazelnuts, although local cooks tend to make it with whatever nuts grow locally in their area. I prefer to use almonds, although all nuts generally work well. ⊕ *Great with grilled and deep-fried foods.*

makes 1¼ cups

3 thick slices of white bread, crusts removed

⅓ cup whole milk

1 heaping cup almonds (or any other
    good-quality nuts)

3 garlic cloves, crushed

½ cup olive oil

salt and freshly cracked black pepper

juice of 1 lemon

1 Put the bread in a bowl, cover with the milk, and let soak for 30 minutes.

2 Transfer to a blender, add the almonds and garlic, and blitz to a paste.

3 Using the feeder tube, pour in the oil in a thin stream with the motor running, to form an emulsion. Season and add lemon juice to taste.

TAHINI SAUCE

⊕ *This famous Middle Eastern sauce is great not only as a dip to serve with falafel, but also as a wonderful dressing for my bean, mint, and chickpea salad (see below).*

makes 1¼ cups

⅔ cup tahini (sesame seed paste)

3 garlic cloves, crushed

juice of 1 lemon

1 teaspoon ground cumin

a pinch each of cayenne pepper, ground coriander,
    and ground cardamom

¼–½ cup hot water

salt

1 Put the tahini and garlic in a blender and add the lemon juice and spices.

2 Slowly add the hot water through the feeder tube, with the motor running, until the sauce has a dropping consistency. Season and transfer to a bowl.

Variations

Finish the sauce with ¼ cup thick, plain yogurt and 2 tablespoons chopped mint: fantastic with grilled eggplant slices.

Add some zip with a little chopped red chile or Tabasco sauce.

GREEN BEAN, MINT, AND CHICKPEA SALAD (for 4 people)

Put 11 ounces cooked green beans and 14 ounces canned or cooked dried chickpeas in a bowl with a handful of mint leaves. Add salt, pepper, and lemon juice to taste. Stir in ¼ cup tahini sauce and mix well. Sprinkle some more mint leaves on top and serve at room temperature.

ZHOUG

A hot and extremely fragrant chile-pepper sauce from the Yemen. ⊕ *Wonderful with meat, fish, and poultry; I also like to add it to vegetable broths. It is sometimes made with red chile, but I prefer the flavor of green here.*

makes 1¼ cups

10 green jalapeño chiles, seeded
4 garlic cloves, crushed
a good bunch of flat-leaf parsley
a good bunch of cilantro leaves
1 teaspoon ground cumin
½ teaspoon ground coriander
a pinch of cayenne pepper
⅓ cup olive oil
salt and freshly cracked black pepper

1 Put the chiles and garlic in a blender and blitz until smooth.
2 Add the herbs, spices, and enough water to blitz into a smooth paste.
3 Add the olive oil, season to taste, and blitz for a final minute.
4 Transfer the sauce to a bowl, cover, and refrigerate until ready to use. It will keep in the fridge for up to 3 months.

PG tip Shatta, another Middle Eastern hot sauce, is prepared in the same way, but with milder, red chiles, which results in a slightly milder flavor. Great for giving a salad dressing a lift.

HARISSA

This spiced red chile sauce is found throughout the Maghreb, especially in Tunisia and Morocco. In Algeria it is also known as dersa. It is served alongside almost everything savory—from tagines to grilled fish, or just simply as a dip in which to immerse chunks of crusty bread. Although there are some good varieties of ready-made harissa now available, there are just as many that are poorly made, so it's always better to make your own. It lasts for up to 1 month in the fridge, or 3 months in the freezer.

makes 1½ cups

5 red jalapeño chiles, roughly chopped

1 cup canned plum tomatoes

3 garlic cloves, crushed

1 tablespoon tomato paste

1 tablespoon ground cumin

2 teaspoons hot curry powder

1 teaspoon ground caraway

1 teaspoon ground coriander

½ teaspoon cayenne pepper

3½ tablespoons olive oil

a dash of vinegar

a pinch of coarse salt

1 Put all the ingredients except the vinegar and salt in a blender and blitz to a smooth, thickish paste.

2 Transfer to a bowl and add the vinegar and salt.

LAMB AND MERGUEZ BROCHETTES WITH SQUASH AND MINT COUSCOUS

In this tasty lamb dish the harissa is used as a marinade for the meat. For those who enjoy the adrenalin pleasures of hot food, serve a little harissa with the dish as well.

serves 4

4 trimmed lamb sirloin chops, 7 ounces each, cut into large cubes

6 ounces merguez sausages, thickly sliced

2 tablespoons harissa (see left)

juice of ½ lemon

1 tablespoon olive oil

for the couscous

14 ounces peeled butternut squash, cut into cubes

1 cup couscous

1 cup hot chicken stock (see page 9)

4 tablespoons chopped mint leaves

2 tablespoons olive oil

a pinch of ground cumin

salt and freshly cracked black pepper

saffron-infused plain yogurt, for serving

1 Put the lamb and merguez in a bowl and add the harissa, lemon juice, oil, and some salt. Let it stand, covered, at room temperature for 1 hour.

2 Thread alternate cubes of lamb and merguez onto 4 pre-soaked wooden skewers.

3 Preheat a barbecue or grill pan and cook for 6–8 minutes until the meat is charred all over but pink in the middle, and turn them regularly as they cook.

4 Meanwhile, cook the squash on a skewer on the barbecue or in the grill pan until lightly charred and tender.

5 Put the couscous in a bowl and add the hot stock, then cover with plastic wrap and let stand for 2–3 minutes. Remove the plastic and fluff up the grains with a fork. Add the grilled squash, mint, oil, cumin, and salt and pepper to taste.

6 Serve the meat on top of the couscous, with the saffron yogurt.

MESHWIYA

Tunisia's answer to the Mexican salsa, hot and heady, but at the same time fresh and lively.

⊕ *Serve it with a spice-roasted leg of lamb or grilled lamb chops, but on a hot summer's day spread it on thick slices of baguette while the barbecue is heating up!*

makes ⅔ cup

3 ripe but firm plum tomatoes, chopped into small
   pieces
1 large red pepper, roasted, seeded, and chopped
   into small pieces
1 teaspoon harissa (see page 98)
2 garlic cloves, crushed
1 teaspoon ground cumin
2 tablespoons olive oil
juice of ½ lemon
2 tablespoons chopped flat-leaf parsley
salt and freshly cracked black pepper

1 Heat a dry frying pan over medium heat, then add the tomatoes and red pepper and cook for 1 minute, or until the tomatoes are just beginning to soften. Add the harissa and cook for another minute.
2 Transfer to a bowl and add the remaining ingredients. Mix well, season to taste, and serve at room temperature.

THE AMERICAS

There is a saying, "Taste a country's cuisine and you will taste its culture." Nowhere is this more apparent than in the countries of South America and the Caribbean. There, they reject the traditional, dairy-based sauces of France and Europe in favor of light, piquant salsas and relishes, highly flavored with chiles, limes, herbs, and spices. These ingredients not only add taste, texture, and color but also make a bold and exciting statement. They stimulate the eye while enlivening the palate. Furthermore, they are simple to prepare and extremely healthy.

It's almost impossible to imagine a meal without sauces in the Americas. In Mexico, breakfast eggs are invariably accompanied by a bowl of salsa fresca, an uncooked tomato relish, while in the evening more complex sauces, made of toasted and ground dried chiles and spices, are enjoyed. In the Caribbean, there are the Creole sauces popular in the French-speaking islands, or the sofrito of Spanish-speaking islands such as Cuba. Sauces like these are also found in the Deep South of the United States, which has strong historical links with the Caribbean.

CREOLE SAUCE

A classic most Creole locals know as "red gravy," this is the basis for the famous shrimp Creole or any fish dish that calls for a lightly spiced red sauce. Like many sauces from this region, it begins with a little "holy trinity" of sautéed onion, celery, and bell pepper. ⊕ *It works well with any firm fish such as snapper or monkfish (angler fish).*

makes about 3 cups

2 tablespoons unsalted butter

1 tablespoon olive oil

1 onion, chopped

2 stalks of celery, thinly sliced

2 garlic cloves, crushed

1 green bell pepper, seeded and cut into
   ¾-inch pieces

½ teaspoon ground cumin

½ teaspoon oregano leaves

1 tablespoon tomato paste

1 teaspoon white wine vinegar

1¼ cups chicken stock (see page 9)

¼ cup dry white wine

1 teaspoon Worcestershire sauce

2 tablespoons chopped flat-leaf parsley

1 bay leaf

salt and a pinch of chili powder

1 Heat the butter and oil in a pan, then add the onion, celery, garlic, and green pepper. Cook over a low heat until softened and with just a little color.

2 Add the cumin and oregano and cook for another minute.

3 Stir in the tomato paste and cook for 2 minutes more.

4 Add the vinegar, stock, wine, Worcestershire sauce, parsley, and bay leaf. Mix well, then cook for 2–3 minutes. Season with salt and chili powder.

CREOLE SNAPPER WITH CRISPY SPICY ONIONS

serves 4

4 snapper fillets, 6 ounces each, cut in
   half lengthwise

juice of 2 limes

1 garlic clove, crushed

salt and freshly cracked black pepper

2 tablespoons olive oil

1 cup creole sauce (see left)

for the onions

1 tablespoon Cajun spices

1 tablespoon flour

2 onions, thinly sliced and separated into rings

2 tablespoons whole milk

oil, for deep-frying

flat-leaf parsley, for serving

1 Place the fish in a non-reactive dish, toss gently with the lime juice, garlic, and some salt and pepper, and let it marinate for 30 minutes. Remove and dry on paper towels.

2 Heat the oil in a frying pan and, when it is hot, add the fish and fry for 1–2 minutes on each side, until golden. Remove to a plate. Add the creole sauce to the pan, top with the fish, cover, and lightly braise for 4–5 minutes.

3 Meanwhile, to make the crispy onions, mix the Cajun spices and flour together in a bowl. Dip the onions into the milk, then into the flour and spice mixture, shaking off any excess.

4 Deep-fry in hot oil (325°F) until crisp and golden, then drain on paper towels.

5 Spoon the fish and sauce onto a serving dish, top with the spicy onions, and serve garnished with flat-leaf parsley.

MEXICAN SALSA VERDE

The following two sauces, green and red, are perhaps the staple of the Mexican kitchen: one or the other seems to accompany almost every meal. Salsa verde can be made either roasted or raw; it's up to your personal taste, so I am giving my favorite, the roasted version.

Salsa roja is traditionally roasted and therefore tends to be the more heady of the two. Both versions are poured over meat, fish, or egg dishes.

You can use a mortar and pestle rather than a blender for the first two steps of this recipe if you prefer.

PG tip – a note on chiles
Serrano chiles are sold red or mature green, moderate to very hot, with an intense bite. They are often used in Thai cooking, but are more synonymous with Mexico and the southwestern United States. Jalapeño (pronounced halapenyo) chiles are green when matured, hot with an immediate bite. They are sold fresh, canned, or pickled.

Both serrano and jalapeño chiles can be bought from spice shops and some good supermarkets. If they are unavailable, any good hot green chile will be fine.

makes about 1 cup

2 green serrano chiles

1 green jalapeño chile

6 fresh tomatillos or small green tomatoes, cut in half

1 small onion, chopped

2 garlic cloves, crushed

a few small handfuls of cilantro leaves

salt and a good pinch of ground cumin

1 In a dry frying pan, toast the chiles, stirring for 1 minute until aromatic and lightly charred with darkened spots. Transfer to a blender.

2 Add the tomatillos to the same dry pan and fry until charred, then add to the blender.

3 Add the onion, garlic, and cilantro to the blender. Blitz with enough water to form a sauce-like consistency.

4 Season with salt and cumin.The salsa will keep well for several days in the fridge.

SALSA ROJA

The endless varieties of chile in Mexico bring different qualities to food: the nuttiness of cascabel, the searing heat of de árbol, and the smokiness of the red chipotle variety, but any dried chile will give you the required punch. This sauce is also often known as enchilada sauce.

makes about 1 cup

⅓ ounce small, hot, dried chiles (de árbol or ancho)

4 garlic cloves, unpeeled

4 ripe but firm plum tomatoes, cut in half

½ teaspoon sugar

½ teaspoon dried oregano

1 tablespoon vegetable oil

a good pinch of ground cumin

salt

1 In a dry frying pan, toast the chiles, stirring for 1 minute until they become aromatic and lightly charred with darkened spots. Transfer to a bowl, cover with hot water, and let soak for 30 minutes.
2 In the same pan, toast the garlic, turning often, until softened and darkened in places, about 15 minutes. Let cool, then peel.
3 Add the tomatoes to the same pan and dry-fry over a low heat until charred, about 5 minutes each side. Transfer to a blender.
4 Drain the soaked chiles and add to the tomatoes in the blender. Blitz, adding enough water to give a sauce-like consistency.
5 Add the sugar, oregano, oil, cumin, and a little salt, then blitz for another 30 seconds. The salsa will keep well for several days in the fridge.

SALSA FRESCA

(or salsa cruda)

The simplest of table sauces in Mexican cuisine; every family has their own particular favorite. It is fresh-tasting and extremely addictive. Salsas are a great time-saver in the kitchen: incredibly easy to make, and perfect with eggs, beans, tortilla chips, shellfish, and poultry dishes. For utmost freshness, don't make them too far in advance, and use them as soon as possible after they have infused. The red chiles can be replaced with green or yellow varieties.

makes about 1 cup

11 ounces ripe but firm vine tomatoes, cut into small pieces

1 red onion, cut into small pieces

2 red jalapeño chiles, finely chopped

1 tablespoon sugar or maple syrup

juice of 3 limes

2 garlic cloves, crushed

2 tablespoons each chopped oregano and cilantro

1 Mix all the ingredients together in a bowl and let infuse for at least 30 minutes before using.

Variations

In certain parts of Mexico, spices such as ground cumin or cayenne pepper, and herbs such as oregano are added to the salsas; variations are limitless, so add whatever herb or spice you feel will work well.

PICO DE GALLO

Literally translating as "rooster's beak," this is a similar, but hotter, Mexican table sauce, using the same recipe but with the chiles char-grilled before being chopped and with 2 tablespoons distilled white vinegar instead of the lime juice.

MEXICAN
SALSA VERDE
If you can't find tomatillos,
green tomatoes are an
acceptable substitute, but
they do not have the apple-
and-lemon tartness of
tomatillos.

PG tip
Limes can sometimes be
a bit hard and the juice
difficult to extract. In this
case, simply place in a
microwave for 10 seconds
(no longer or the juice will
get very hot) to loosen the
juices from within.

CHIMOL

This is a fresh, simple, and tasty sauce from El Salvador. ● *I love it with cumin-rubbed flank steak cooked on the barbecue, and also spooned over marinated goat cheese crushed onto tortilla chips.*

makes about ¾–1 cup

4 vine tomatoes, cut in half

2 tablespoons olive oil

a good bunch of cilantro

juice of 2 limes

3 tablespoons chopped mint leaves

1 small red onion, finely chopped

4 red radishes, finely chopped

½ teaspoon ground cumin

a pinch of dried red pepper flakes

salt

1 Heat a grill pan until hot. Brush the tomato halves with the olive oil and cook on the grill pan until lightly charred and softened.

2 Meanwhile, combine all the remaining ingredients in a bowl, with salt to taste.

3 Mash the grilled tomatoes into the bowl and mix thoroughly. Adjust the seasoning and let stand for 30 minutes, to infuse, before serving.

AJILIMOJILI

A hot garlic, pepper, and chile sauce from Puerto Rico. ● *Excellent served with roast pork or used as a marinade for meat and fish.*

makes 1¼ cups

3 hot red chiles (preferably serrano), seeded and chopped

2 red bell peppers, cut in half, seeded, and roughly chopped

4 black peppercorns

4 garlic cloves

salt

juice of 4 limes

⅓ cup olive oil

3 tablespoons chopped cilantro

1 Put the chiles and red peppers in a mortar (or blender) with the peppercorns, garlic, and some salt, and pound (or blitz) to a paste.

2 Add the lime juice and oil and work (or blitz) to a puree. The finished sauce will keep for up to 1 week in a sealed container in the fridge.

MEXICAN RED MOLE

Mole (pronounced mo-lay), from the Spanish word for "to grind," is Mexico's national dish, which may surprise you if your experience of Mexican cooking extends no further than enchiladas or burritos. Every Mexican home has its favorite mole recipe, and there are countless versions. They always contain ground seeds or nuts and, of course, chiles, and are usually served with chicken or meat. This red mole offers a sauce of sweetness, a little bitterness, nuttiness, and earthiness all at once, if you can imagine it.

Don't be put off by the long ingredients list; mole is worth the time it takes to make. Crisp corn tortillas are available from the Mexican foods section of your supermarket; do not use flour tortillas, as they are completely different.

makes 4 cups

2 dried ancho chiles

2 dried pasilla chiles or ½ teaspoon dried
   red pepper flakes

3 cups chicken stock (see page 9)

2 crisp corn tortillas, 6–7-inch diameter

1 tablespoon lard or vegetable oil

1 onion, chopped

½ teaspoon dried oregano

2 garlic cloves, crushed

14½-ounce can tomatoes

⅓ cup raisins, soaked in water until plump,
   then drained

2½ ounces dark unsweetened Mexican chocolate
   (see tip, right)

2 tablespoons peanut butter

1 tablespoon white wine vinegar

1 teaspoon sugar

½ teaspoon ground cinnamon

½ teaspoon ground cloves

1 teaspoon coriander seeds

1 tablespoon sesame seeds, toasted

a pinch of ground anise

salt

1 Heat a dry frying pan, then add the chiles and dry-fry until fragrant and charred in places. Transfer to a bowl, cover with water, and let soak for 30 minutes.

2 Pour 1 cup of the chicken stock into a pan and bring to a boil. Add the tortillas, then remove from the heat.

3 Heat half the lard or oil in a separate pan and add the onion, oregano, and garlic. Cook for 3–4 minutes until softened.

4 Remove the chiles from the water and roughly chop. Add to the onions in the pan and cook for 30 seconds.

5 Pour in the tortilla-infused stock (the tortillas will have dissolved into the stock by now) and bring to a boil.

6 Add the tomatoes and a little salt, along with the rest of the ingredients except for the stock, then transfer the mixture to a blender and blitz until smooth.

7 Return to the pan, add the remaining stock, and simmer for 12–15 minutes.

SIMPLE RED MOLE CHICKEN

Sear some chicken pieces in a flameproof and ovenproof pan until golden all over. Pour the red mole sauce over the chicken, cover with a lid or foil, and bake in the oven at 375°F for 45 minutes or until the chicken is cooked. Sprinkle with a few toasted sesame seeds before serving.

PG tip Mexican chocolate differs from the sort commonly found in Europe or America; some types are very sweet while others have no sweetening at all. It is often flavored, with some brands containing cinnamon. If you are traveling in Mexico, look out for chocolate from Oaxaca or Puebla, and bring some home! Otherwise, just use chocolate with the highest possible percentage of cocoa solids—at least 70 percent.

MOJO CRIOLLO

Mojo is the collective name of several hot sauces and relishes which originated in the Canary Islands. Basically consisting of olive oil, garlic, chile, and cumin, with an acid component such as vinegar or lemon, they are served at the beginning of a meal.

Somewhat similar-style mojos can be found in the Caribbean and in Cuba, where they are the national table sauce—mojo is to Cuban cuisine what salsa is to Mexican and vinaigrettes are to French. This recipe is for perhaps the most famous of all mojos. ⊕ *Serve with just about anything; grilled fish and meat are especially good. Mojos taste best when served a couple of hours after they are made.*

makes 1¼ cups

5 tablespoons olive oil

2 garlic cloves, crushed

½ cup sour (Seville) orange juice or equal mixture of lime juice and orange juice

1 teaspoon cumin seeds

1 hot red chile, seeded and finely chopped

1 teaspoon sherry vinegar (optional)

1 tablespoon tomato ketchup (optional)

salt and freshly cracked black pepper

1 Put the oil and garlic in a pan and heat gently until lightly golden but not browned, about 30 seconds.

2 Add the orange juice or lime and orange juice mixture, the cumin and chile, bring to a boil, and simmer for 3–4 minutes until slightly reduced.

3 Remove from the heat and let cool slightly before adding the vinegar and ketchup, if using. Season to taste, and let infuse for a couple of hours before serving. Mojo will keep, covered, in the fridge for up to 2 days.

Variations

MOJO DE AJO (garlic mojo)

Replace the chile with pickled red chiles and add double the amount of garlic (4 cloves). When the mixture is cool, add 2 tablespoons chopped flat-leaf parsley.

RED ONION, GRAPEFRUIT, AND CILANTRO MOJO

Proceed as for the basic recipe, but replace the orange juice with grapefruit juice and add ½ small chopped red onion and a few chopped cilantro leaves at the end before cooling. Ideal with freshly flaked crabmeat.

MANGO AND MINT MOJO

Add ½ chopped fresh mango and 2 tablespoons roughly chopped mint leaves to the basic mojo recipe. Fantastic with lamb chops.

PERUVIAN AJÍ SAUCE

A green dipping sauce from Peru, where ají denotes a hot variety of chile. ⊕ *It is fantastic with small steamed shrimp.*

makes 1 cup

1 green jalapeño chile

½ head of romaine lettuce

½ cup mayonnaise (see page 30)

2 slices of white bread, crusts removed, soaked in
   3½ tablespoons water

a good handful of cilantro leaves

1 Heat a dry frying pan over medium heat, add the chile, and dry-fry until charred all over, about 2–3 minutes. Remove and let cool.

2 Remove the center core from the lettuce and cut the remaining leaves into small pieces.

3 Put the lettuce and roasted chiles in a blender along with the mayonnaise and blitz to a puree.

4 Squeeze the excess moisture from the bread and add to the blender along with the cilantro. Blitz to a smooth puree. The finished sauce will keep, covered, for up to 2 days in the fridge.

SALSA DE MANI

⊕ *In Ecuador, this creamy peanut sauce usually accompanies the popular deep-fried potato croquettes. It is also wonderful when used as a base for braised chicken (see below).*

makes 2½ cups

2 tablespoons olive oil

1 onion, finely chopped

2 garlic cloves, crushed

1 large red bell pepper, cut in half, seeded, and cut
   into strips

1 teaspoon ground cumin

½ teaspoon dried oregano

1 tablespoon tomato paste

14 ounces canned tomatoes

3 tablespoons smooth peanut butter

salt and freshly cracked black pepper

1 Heat the oil in a pan, add the onion, garlic, and red pepper, and cook for 3–5 minutes until the vegetables begin to soften.

2 Add the cumin, oregano, tomato paste, and tomatoes, and bring to a boil. Cook for 8–10 minutes until the sauce becomes flavorful and thickened.

3 Stir in the peanut butter, season to taste, and cook for another 5 minutes. The sauce will keep in the fridge, covered, for 2–3 days.

BRAISED CHICKEN WITH CREAMED PEANUTS AND TOMATOES
(for 4 people)

Cut up a 3½–4-pound free-range chicken and season with salt and pepper. Fry the pieces in 2 tablespoons hot vegetable oil for 5–6 minutes, turning a few times, until golden all over. Add 2½ cups salsa de mani along with 1 cup chicken stock (see page 9) and mix well. Cover and simmer for another 12–15 minutes until the chicken is cooked and tender.

SALSA RANCHERO

Salsa means sauce in Spanish, and in Latin America it is generally an uncooked mixture of chiles and tomatoes. ⊕ *This chunky version has a great affinity with egg dishes, but also with chicken and fish. It is not overly hot and can be enjoyed by those who do not care for sauces that raise your temperature!*

makes 1¼ cups

2 tablespoons vegetable oil

1 onion, finely chopped

3 garlic cloves

1 red jalapeño chile, chopped

6 ripe but firm tomatoes, chopped (or 1 cup canned)

1 teaspoon tomato paste

a pinch of sugar

1 teaspoon ground cumin

1 teaspoon chopped oregano

1 tablespoon chopped cilantro

1 Heat the oil in a pan, add the onion, garlic, and chile, and cook for 8–10 minutes, until softened.
2 Add the tomatoes, tomato paste, sugar, cumin, oregano, and cilantro, and simmer over a low heat for 10–12 minutes, for the flavors to infuse.
3 Remove from the heat and let cool. The sauce will keep, covered, in the fridge for 2–3 days.

HUEVOS RANCHEROS

I first enjoyed this dish of Mexican ranch-style eggs in Texas, while staying at The Mansion on Turtle Creek about 15 years ago. I was introduced to it by the then chef, good friend and pioneer of Tex-Mex cooking, Dean Fearing. It soon became a favorite of mine: a great breakfast or light brunch option.

serves 4

4 tablespoons vegetable oil

1 small onion, finely chopped

1 garlic clove, crushed

1 red chile, finely chopped

¾–1 cup cooked black beans, lightly crushed

½ teaspoon ground cumin

4 corn tortillas

4 cage-free eggs

⅓–½ cup guacamole (see tip below)

⅔ cup salsa ranchero (see left), for serving

1 Heat 1 tablespoon of the oil in a pan, add the onion, garlic, and chile, and cook for 2 minutes, without browning them. Add the beans and cumin, and cook until heated through. Remove from the heat and keep warm.
2 Heat 1 teaspoon of the oil in a large frying pan and fry each tortilla, one at a time, and adding more oil as needed, until crisp and golden. Remove, drain on paper towels, and keep warm.
3 Add the remaining oil to the pan and fry the eggs.
4 To serve, place a crisp tortilla on each serving plate and top with fried beans. Top each with a fried egg and a good spoonful of guacamole. Spoon over the salsa ranchero on top and serve.

PG tip – guacamole
Cut 1 large ripe avocado in half and remove the pit. Scoop the flesh into a bowl and mash lightly with a fork, leaving a few lumps. Stir in ½ red onion, finely chopped, 1 green chile, seeded and finely chopped, 1 ounce chopped cilantro, 1 seeded and finely chopped ripe tomato, 2 tablespoons lime juice, and salt to taste. Use immediately, or cover with plastic wrap to prevent the avocado turning brown.

SIMPLE CAJUN KETCHUP

Everyone loves ketchup smothered over a burger or crispy fries. You just can't beat it—sweet and toothsome. The addition of a little heat via some Cajun spices adds another flavor dimension.

makes 1¼ cups

1 tablespoon olive oil

1 large onion, finely chopped

8 very ripe, sweet tomatoes, seeded and
    roughly chopped

¼ cup soft brown sugar

2 tablespoons black treacle or molasses

3 tablespoons white wine vinegar or cider vinegar

2 tablespoons tomato paste

½ teaspoon powdered mustard

1 tablespoon Cajun spices

juice of ½ lemon

salt and freshly cracked black pepper

1 Heat the oil in a pan until very hot. Add the onion and tomatoes, cover, and let cook over a high heat for 3–4 minutes.

2 Add the remaining ingredients, except the lemon juice and seasoning, lower the heat, and cook, uncovered, for 25 minutes, stirring occasionally.

3 Remove from the heat and add the lemon juice. Transfer to a blender and blitz until smooth (for a really smooth ketchup, strain it through a fine mesh strainer, too).

4 Season with salt and pepper, then let cool completely before serving. Alternatively, keep in the fridge until needed, for up to 1 month.

PG tip If you can't buy Cajun spices, make your own: in a mortar and pestle, crush to a fairly fine powder 1 teaspoon each of chopped garlic, cayenne pepper, paprika, dried thyme, and dried oregano, and a little salt and pepper.

PEBRE SAUCE

In Chile, this hot sauce accompanies just about everything. The heat varies from one cook to another, with some versions only mildly hot, and others leading you to seek solace in a cool drink. This recipe is the way I like it: not too hot, but with purpose.

makes 1¼ cups

2 small hot red chiles (or ½ teaspoon
    Tabasco sauce)
½ cup olive oil
1 onion, finely chopped
2 tablespoons chopped cilantro
2 tablespoons chopped flat-leaf parsley
3 garlic cloves, crushed
1 teaspoon oregano
¼ cup red wine vinegar
salt and freshly cracked black pepper

1 Put the chiles with half the oil in a blender and blitz to a puree. Transfer to a bowl.
2 Add the remaining ingredients and adjust the seasoning to taste. Leave it covered for 2 hours at room temperature for the flavors to infuse. The sauce will keep in the fridge, covered, for up to 3 days, but is at its best eaten on the day it is made.

SOFRITO

Sofrito is one of the cornerstones and treasures of Spanish Caribbean cuisine, the smell of sautéed onions, garlic, and peppers pervading from homes everywhere. ● *Use as a base for soups, stews, and rice dishes, much as for the Italian version, soffrito. It also makes a great topping for pizzas or crostini.*

makes 1½ cups

2 tablespoons olive oil or melted pork fat
1 onion, finely chopped
3 garlic cloves, crushed
2 red bell peppers, cut in half, seeded, and
    finely chopped
½ teaspoon ground cumin
½ teaspoon dried oregano
1 bay leaf
1 cup canned tomatoes, finely chopped
salt and freshly cracked black pepper
2 tablespoons chopped cilantro

1 Heat the oil in a nonstick frying pan and add the onion, garlic, red peppers, cumin, oregano, and bay leaf. Cook over a low heat for 5–6 minutes until softened.
2 Add the tomatoes along with some salt and pepper, and cook slowly until reduced and thickened. Stir in the cilantro and season with a little extra cumin, if you like. Sofrito will keep, refrigerated, for 3–4 days.

SALSA GUASACACA

⊕ *A colorful Venezuelan variation of guacamole, traditionally served with grilled meats. I also love it with hard-boiled eggs.*

makes about 1 cup

1 large, ripe avocado (preferably Hass)

¼ cup olive oil

1 garlic clove, crushed

2 tablespoons red wine vinegar

½ teaspoon hot red chili sauce (or 1 hot red chile, finely chopped)

salt and freshly cracked black pepper

2 vine tomatoes, seeded and cut into ¼-inch pieces

1 small green bell pepper, cut in half, seeded, and finely chopped

1 small red bell pepper, cut in half, seeded, and finely chopped

2 cage-free eggs, hard-boiled, peeled, and chopped

1 tablespoon chopped flat-leaf parsley

1 tablespoon chopped cilantro

1 Cut the avocado in half and remove the pit and skin. Mash one half and set aside. Chop the other half into small pieces.

2 In a bowl, mix the oil, garlic, vinegar, chili sauce or chile, and salt and pepper.

3 Add the tomatoes, green and red peppers, eggs, herbs, and chopped avocado. Gently mix together.

4 Fold in the mashed avocado, adjust the seasoning to taste, and serve.

MINT CHIMICHURRI

Classic chimichurri is the ultimate companion for steak throughout Argentina, though I first tasted it smeared generously over smoked brisket and tucked up in a soft hamburger bun at a barbecue in Houston, Texas. It certainly made an impression and now regularly appears on my menus. It could be described, I suppose, as Latin America's answer to pesto. Traditionally, only parsley and oregano are used, but here is my favorite variation on the theme, using mint. For the traditional version, omit the mint and use double the quantity of parsley.

⊕ *The minty sauce makes a great marinade for steaks and vegetables.*

makes 1¼ cups

1 bunch of mint leaves

1 small bunch of flat-leaf parsley

1 teaspoon dried red pepper flakes

3 garlic cloves, crushed

⅓ cup plus 1 tablespoon mild olive oil

¼ cup water

3 tablespoons red wine vinegar

1 teaspoon dried oregano

salt and freshly cracked black pepper

4 plum tomatoes, peeled, seeded, and chopped (optional)

1 Put the mint and parsley in a blender, add the red pepper flakes and garlic, and blitz until fine.

2 Add the oil, water, vinegar, oregano, and a little salt and pepper, then blitz until slightly coarse. Add the tomatoes, if using.

3 Let the sauce stand for a few hours before serving. It will keep in the fridge, in a screw-top jar, for 2–3 days, but is at its best when freshly made.

SAUCE CHIEN

(dog sauce)

I first encountered this bizarrely named sauce many years ago at the famous La Sammana Resort Hotel on the island of St. Maarten in the Caribbean. The chef served it spooned over grilled fish and vegetables, but never could tell me how it got its name! My research since then suggests that it is named after the numerous packs of wild dogs that roam the island. In essence it is similar to a French vinaigrette but with the spirit and character of the French West Indies.

makes ⅔ cup

2 garlic cloves, crushed

1 hot red chile (habañero or Scotch bonnet)

2 shallots, finely chopped

3 scallions, finely chopped

3 tablespoons chopped cilantro

2 tablespoons chopped flat-leaf parsley

½ teaspoon chopped thyme leaves

salt and freshly cracked black pepper

juice of 2 limes

3½ tablespoons olive oil

3 tablespoons boiling water

1 In a bowl, mix the garlic, chile, shallots, scallions, herbs, and some salt and pepper.

2 Add the lime juice and whisk in the oil.

3 Add the boiling water and whisk to form a light emulsion, then adjust the seasoning. Let it infuse for 1 hour before using. The sauce can be kept for 2 days, in a sealed container in the fridge.

CAESAR DRESSING

This classic dressing was first created in 1924 in Mexico, by the Italian chef Caesar Cardini at his restaurant in Tijuana. It has now emerged as an international icon, showing up in casual as well as ritzy restaurants the world over.

The art of making a great Caesar dressing, and salad for that matter, is to strike the right balance: too much garlic is overpowering, for instance.

Those of you who are not fans of anchovies might like to know that the original recipe did not in fact include them. Sorry to say that mine does!

makes 1 cup

1 large cage-free egg

1 teaspoon Worcestershire sauce

juice of ½ lemon

1 garlic clove, crushed

4 salted anchovies, rinsed, dried, and finely chopped

1 teaspoon superfine capers, rinsed and chopped

1 teaspoon Dijon mustard

freshly cracked black pepper

⅓ cup extra virgin olive oil

1½ ounces Parmesan cheese (preferably Reggiano), finely grated

1 Immerse the egg in boiling water for 1 minute. Remove and let cool.

2 Mix the Worcestershire sauce, lemon juice, garlic, anchovies, capers, and mustard in a bowl. Season with pepper.

3 Crack the egg into the bowl and whisk until smooth. Slowly trickle in the oil in a steady stream, whisking until smooth and emulsified. Do not add the oil too quickly or the sauce will separate.

4 Stir in the grated Parmesan and serve.

Variation

ROQUEFORT CAESAR DRESSING

Replace the Parmesan with crumbled Roquefort cheese.

TROPICAL ISLAND CHUTNEY

This is more of a sauce than a chutney, but made along the same lines. A lot of New World sauces include fruit, which is not surprising given how abundant fruit is in this part of the world.

makes 1½ cups

⅔ cup cider vinegar

¼ cup sugar

2 tablespoons dark brown sugar

1 red onion, finely chopped

1 hot red chile, seeded and chopped

1-inch piece of fresh ginger, peeled and grated

½ teaspoon ground cinnamon

½ teaspoon ground allspice

⅓ cup golden raisins

1 ripe mango, peeled and cut into small pieces

5 ounces fresh pineapple, peeled and cut into small pieces

1 guava, peeled and cut into small pieces

1 banana, peeled and cut into small pieces

2 teaspoons chopped cilantro (optional)

1 Put the vinegar and both sugars in a heavy pan and bring slowly to a boil. Add the onion, chile, ginger, and spices, and cook for another 10 minutes.

2 Add the raisins and chopped fruits and cook over a low heat for a final 15 minutes. Let cool, and add the cilantro, if using, before serving.

XNIPEC SALSA

This is a sweet-and-sour habañero chile salsa from the Yucatán peninsula in Mexico. Habañero, usually red or yellow, is an extremely fiery chile, often confused with the infamous Scotch bonnet, which is also lantern-shaped. Despite its intense heat it has a fruity tone that goes particularly well with fruits and tomatoes. Use it sparingly, and take care when handling it. If you prefer, use milder chiles.

⊕ *Lovely with grilled fish or chicken.*

makes ⅔ cup

1 red onion, chopped

3 ripe vine tomatoes, peeled, seeded, and chopped

1 habañero chile (or other red chile), seeded and chopped

scant ½ cup fresh bitter (Seville) orange juice or equal mixture of lime juice and orange juice

salt

1 Combine all the ingredients in a bowl, with salt to taste, and leave for 30 minutes, for the flavors to infuse.

PG tip Seville oranges (bitter oranges) are not widely available but may sometimes be found in Caribbean grocery stores. If you can't find them, use ordinary oranges, but add a little lime juice to give that sour effect.

ASIA

The sauces of Asia are usually based on a few simple ingredients and are quick and easy to prepare. Throughout the region you'll find a plethora of dipping sauces placed on practically every table, both in the home and in restaurants. They make a wonderful accompaniment to finger foods such as crisp spring rolls and grilled spiced meat satays, or spooned over local delicacies such as seafood and fish salads. These sauces may have a thin consistency but are full of spice and savor. Extremely versatile, they can be used to enliven a simple dish of noodles or rice, and make everyday meals memorable. They are also a boon for the busy cook, as they require little, if any, cooking and often rely on ingredients already in store.

Some Asian sauces form an integral part of the dish and are slightly more complex. Thai, Malaysian, and Indian curry sauces, for example, require a spice paste to be prepared first by roasting and pounding spices and aromatics; the paste is then added to coconut milk or stock and used for cooking meat, fish, or vegetables. Like the simplest of dipping sauces, however, these cooking sauces are always characterized by clear, vibrant flavors.

BALINESE DARK SOY SAUCE

A fiery-hot, salty sauce that will enliven the palate, with shades of licorice from the kecap manis.

⊕ *Serve with satays or use as a dressing for seafood salad.*

makes ⅔ cup

½ garlic clove, peeled

3 tablespoons vegetable oil

1 teaspoon finely chopped lemongrass

2 scallions, finely chopped

¼ cup kecap manis (Indonesian soy sauce)

1 hot red chile, finely chopped

1 teaspoon distilled white vinegar

1 Pound the garlic in a mortar to a paste.

2 Heat the oil in a small frying pan, add the pounded garlic, stir-fry for 1–2 seconds, then transfer to a small bowl.

3 Add the remaining ingredients to the bowl and let stand for 15 minutes for the flavors to infuse.

PG tip Kecap manis is a sweet-based soy sauce, almost licorice in flavor. It is used widely in Indonesian cooking, and as a seasoning or condiment. If you can't find it, combine equal quantities of light soy sauce and treacle with a good pinch of ground star anise and reduce in a pan until lightly thickened.

SRIRACHA SAUCE

Sriracha is the generic name for the hot sauce adorning every Southeast Asian restaurant table. Like many sauces of the region, it has a perfect balance of sweetness and spice.

Although it started life in a Thai port called Sri Racha, I first encountered the sauce in California, on hot dog stalls and taco stands, served like a ketchup —the perfect accompaniment! Such is its global popularity now that commercial brands are readily available, but it's very simple, and much better, to make your own. ⊕ *It adds a warm glow to seafood such as oysters and clams.*

makes 1½ cups

6 ounces hot red chiles, chopped

1 tablespoon tomato paste

½ cup distilled white vinegar

⅓ cup sugar

6 garlic cloves, crushed

1 cup canned tomatoes

1 Put the chiles and tomato paste in a pan with the vinegar and sugar, and bring to a boil.

2 Add the garlic and tomatoes and cook for 10 minutes.

3 Transfer to a blender and blitz until smooth, then let it go cold before serving. It can be kept in the fridge in a sealed container for up to 1 month.

Variation

COCKTAIL SAUCE

Add 2 tablespoons sriracha to ¼ cup mayonnaise and use for a great Asian-style shrimp cocktail sauce, or serve with fried calamari.

NAM PRIK PHAO

(roasted chili sauce)

🌐 *In Thailand, this fragrant and spicy-hot sauce makes the perfect accompaniment to many dishes: stirred into fried rice with vegetables or seafood or, the way I like it, brushed over grilled fish or shellfish.*

makes 1¼ cups

scant ½ cup vegetable oil
4 shallots, sliced
4 garlic cloves, crushed
8 small dried red chiles
1 tablespoon dried shrimp paste
1 tablespoon palm sugar or brown sugar (optional)
3 tablespoons nam pla (Thai fish sauce)
2 tablespoons tamarind paste
salt

1 Heat the oil in a wok or large frying pan and add the shallots and garlic. Cook until lightly golden, then remove with a slotted spoon to a blender.
2 Add the chiles and shrimp paste to the wok or pan and fry for 1 minute. Remove with a slotted spoon to the blender, reserving the oil in the wok.
3 Add the sugar, if using, to the blender and blitz. Add the nam pla, tamarind, some salt, and the reserved oil from the wok, then blitz again to a blended puree.
4 Transfer to a bowl and let cool. Serve cold. It can be refrigerated for up to three months.

PG tip—a word on fish sauce
Don't be put off by the pungent aroma. Incorporated into a sauce, dressing, or curry, fish sauce becomes less powerful, quite addictive, and a healthy alternative to salt. The Vietnamese (nuoc mam) and Thai (nam pla) versions, made from fermented anchovies, shrimp, or squid, are considered the best and are widely available. Once opened, fish sauce should be refrigerated.

PAN-ROASTED MUSSELS WITH ROASTED CHILI SAUCE

serves 4

2 tablespoons vegetable oil
2 garlic cloves, crushed
2 tablespoons nam prik phao (see left)
2¼ pounds fresh mussels, debearded and cleaned
2 tablespoons nam pla (Thai fish sauce)
scant ½ cup oyster sauce
2 large red chiles, sliced
12 Thai sweet basil leaves
⅔ cup chicken stock (see page 9)
a pinch of sugar, to taste

1 Heat the oil in a wok or large frying pan, add the garlic and nam prik phao, and cook for 30 seconds.
2 Add the mussels in their shells and stir-fry for 1 minute in the sauce.
3 Add the remaining ingredients and cook for another 2–3 minutes, or until the mussels have opened.
4 Divide between 4 bowls and serve with steamed rice.

PG tip When preparing molluscs of any sort, ensure they are closed. Any with open shells are dead and can cause food poisoning. Again, once they are cooked, any remaining closed are dead; discard them, too.

THAI DIPPING SAUCE

I could devour this delicate sweet-and-sour sauce by the gallon. ⊕ *Traditionally served with Thai appetizers such as satays, spring rolls, and spicy fish cakes.*

makes 1¼ cups

¼ cup distilled white vinegar

⅔ cup sugar

½ cup water

1 tablespoon nam pla (Thai fish sauce)

1 small red chile, finely sliced

⅝-inch piece of fresh ginger, peeled and finely chopped (optional)

¾ cup finely chopped cucumber

2 tablespoons chopped roasted peanuts

1 Put the vinegar, sugar, water, nam pla, chile, and ginger, if using, in a pan and bring to a boil.

2 Simmer, uncovered, for 5 minutes or until slightly thickened.

3 Stir in the cucumber and peanuts and serve at room temperature.

CHILE VINEGAR DIPPING SAUCE

This sauce was on almost every table wherever I ate in Thailand, although you will find a version of it throughout Asia; it is a sharply flavored condiment that enlivens any dish. ⊕ *I particularly enjoy it with stir-fried noodles or rice dishes.*

makes ⅔ cup

2 hot red chiles, thinly sliced

scant ½ cup distilled white vinegar

2 teaspoons nam pla (Thai fish sauce)

1 Combine the ingredients in a bowl and let stand for 15 minutes for the flavors to infuse. The dip will keep for 2 weeks in a sealed container in the fridge.

NAM PRIK NOOM

(green chile dipping sauce)

A very hot dip served with sticky rice or grilled vegetables. Charring the ingredients on a barbecue improves the flavor no end, but a grill pan does an acceptable job.

makes 1¼ cups

6 garlic cloves

6 green chiles

3½ ounces large banana shallots, cut in
    half lengthwise

4 ripe, firm tomatoes, seeded and chopped

scant ½ cup vegetable oil

2 tablespoons nam pla (Thai fish sauce)

juice of 2 limes

2 tablespoons chopped cilantro

a good pinch of sugar

1 Heat a dry grill pan over a high heat and add the garlic, chiles, and shallots. Fry for 4–5 minutes, stirring, until fragrant, then let cool before cutting them into small chunks.

2 Transfer to a large mortar along with the tomatoes. Using a pestle, grind to a paste.

3 Add the oil, nam pla, lime juice, cilantro, and sugar, and mix well.

NUOC MAM CHAM

(Vietnamese dipping sauce)

No meal in Vietnam is considered complete without this sauce; it is used as freely as we use salt and pepper. Endless variations are found across Asia, Malaysia, Cambodia, and Thailand. ⊕ *As with all Asian-style dipping sauces, this is great for serving with grilled meat and fish, vegetables, and crispy spring rolls.*

makes ¾–1 cup

½ cup water or coconut juice

2 tablespoons rice wine vinegar

2 tablespoons palm sugar or granulated sugar

2 garlic cloves, crushed

4 hot red chiles, preferably Thai (bird's-eye) chiles,
    finely chopped

1 teaspoon lemon or lime juice

2 tablespoons nuoc mam (Vietnamese fish sauce)

1 Put the water or coconut juice in a small pan with the vinegar and sugar and bring to a boil. Remove from the heat and set aside to cool.

2 Add the garlic, chiles, and lemon or lime juice, then stir in the nuoc mam.

Variations

Add one of the following to the basic sauce: shredded radish or carrots, carrot pickles, chopped cilantro, a little chopped fresh ginger or chopped lemon grass.

NUOC LEO

A cousin of nuoc mam cham; use in the same way. Put 1 tablespoon nuoc mam cham (see above) into a bowl and add ¼ cup hoisin sauce, 3 tablespoons water, 1 tablespoon sweet chili sauce (see page 146), and 2 tablespoons finely ground dry-roasted peanuts. Stir well to mix.

NAM JIM

(green chile and cilantro sauce)

A wonderful dressing, simple and addictive, one of the staples of the Thai kitchen and a great way of learning about the balance of flavor in Thai cooking. There is a number of variations, but the key elements remain the same: hot, sour, salty, and sweet—exemplified here by chile, garlic, lime juice, fish sauce, and palm sugar, all the hallmarks of the country's cuisine. This recipe calls for cilantro roots, but if they are unavailable, just use the leaves. ⊕
Great for enlivening salads, as for my grilled pork and fennel salad, opposite.

makes about 1 cup

1 tablespoon sea salt or kosher salt

3 garlic cloves

3 shallots, chopped

a good handful of cilantro leaves, plus the
    scraped and cleaned roots

4 small hot green chiles, seeded and chopped

3 tablespoons palm sugar or brown sugar

3 tablespoons nam pla (Thai fish sauce)

juice of 8 limes

1 Put the salt, garlic, shallots, and cilantro leaves and roots in a mortar and pestle, and pound until crushed.

2 Add the chiles and sugar and pound again, then remove to a bowl.

3 Add the nam pla and lime juice and mix thoroughly. The dressing should taste hot, sweet, sour, and salty. Add more palm sugar to make it sweeter or more nam pla to make it more salty.

Variations

Replace the green chiles with Dutch or Indonesian lombok chiles, for a slightly less hot version.

SWEET THAI DRESSING

Add 2 tablespoons sweet chili sauce (see page 146) to the basic recipe. Great with grilled beef or calamari salad.

GRILLED PORK NECK WITH FENNEL SALAD

serves 4

1-pound piece of pork neck, cleaned of all fat and
   sinew
1 tablespoon oyster sauce
2 large heads of fennel, outer layer removed
2 tablespoons olive oil
2 large shallots, thinly sliced
¼ cup nam jim (see opposite)
1 handful small mint leaves
2 tablespoons roughly chopped peanuts

1 Place the pork in a steamer set over a pan
of simmering water and steam, covered, for
40 minutes until cooked. Remove to a cutting board
and cut into ½–¾-inch cubes.

2 Put the pork in a bowl or shallow dish and add
the oyster sauce. Mix well and let marinate
for up to 1 hour.

3 Meanwhile, slice the fennel very thinly, using
a kitchen mandoline, if possible, then tip into
ice water.

4 Heat a grill pan until very hot and brush with the
oil. Drain the marinated pork pieces and add them
to the hot pan. Cook for 2–3 minutes on each side,
until lightly browned.

5 Drain and dry the fennel, then put in a bowl with
the shallots. Add the nam jim and toss to mix.

6 Add the grilled pork, toss to coat, then divide the
mixture between 4 individual serving plates.

7 Scatter the mint leaves and peanuts over them
and serve immediately.

ROASTED TOMATO AND GARLIC DIPPING SAUCE

In Laos, many sauces are flavored with garlic, tomato, and peppers and are infused with fresh herbs such as basil, cilantro, and mint.

makes about 1 cup

4 large garlic cloves, unpeeled

3 red chiles, cut in half lengthwise

4 ripe but firm tomatoes, cut in half

1 small red pepper, cut in half and seeded

2 tablespoons vegetable oil

2 tablespoons nam pla (Thai fish sauce)

¼ cup chopped cilantro

2 scallions, finely chopped

2 tablespoons chopped mint

juice of ½ lime

1 Preheat the oven to 400°F. Put the garlic, chiles, tomatoes, and red pepper in an oven dish or roasting pan and drizzle the oil over them.

2 Roast in the oven for 20 minutes, then turn the vegetables and return to the oven for another 20 minutes. Remove from the oven and let cool.

3 When they are cool, slip the roasted garlic cloves from their skin and put in a mortar with the roasted chiles and red pepper. Pound to a coarse paste.

4 Remove and discard the skin from the tomatoes, chop the flesh, and add to the paste, then pound again to a paste.

5 Add the remaining ingredients, mix well, and serve.

PG tip This sauce cannot be made very far in advance, as it relies on the flavor of freshly cooked ingredients. Make it a few hours before you need it, for the best results.

ROASTED TOMATO AND GARLIC DIPPING SAUCE

I particularly like this sauce served with steamed shrimp or fish cooked wrapped in banana leaves, or, during the height of summer, cooked on a hot charcoal barbecue.

SPICE ISLANDS FRUIT SALSA WITH PEANUTS

A wonderful dip for raw vegetables, grilled fish, or meat—easy to make and extremely tasty. Sometimes the sauce is blended to a puree, but I prefer it like this, with each ingredient's flavor shining through individually. ⊕ *Serve with shrimp chips—very addictive!*

makes 1¼ cups

1 tablespoon vegetable oil

4 scallions, finely chopped

1 ripe mango, peeled and chopped

1 kaffir lime leaf

juice of 2 limes

⅔ cup fresh or canned pineapple, cubed

1 tablespoon palm sugar

¾ cup roasted unsalted peanuts, chopped

3 tablespoons chopped cilantro leaves

1 teaspoon sambal oelek (see page 148)

1 Mix all the ingredients in a bowl, adding a little more sambal oelek if you prefer a hotter salsa.

YELLOW PLUM SAUCE

Yellow plum sauce is yet another dipping sauce found in Thailand, traditionally enjoyed with fried foods, such as deep-fried shrimp cakes. Yellow plums have a short season, so enjoy them while you can.

makes about 1 cup

7 ounces yellow plums, pitted and chopped

1 onion, chopped

3 small red chiles, seeded and finely chopped

1-inch piece of fresh ginger, peeled and chopped

½ cup sugar

scant ½ cup distilled white vinegar

scant cup water

juice of 2 limes

a pinch of sea salt or kosher salt

1 Put all the ingredients in a pan and slowly bring to a boil. Reduce the heat a little and gently cook until the plums break down to a jam-like consistency.

2 Let cool and serve at room temperature.

RAITA

A soothing, yogurt-based sauce, ideal to temper hot dishes such as curries. ⊕ *In India it accompanies almost every dish.*

makes ¾–1 cup

7 ounces cucumber

½ teaspoon sea salt or kosher salt

⅔ cup thick plain yogurt

½ teaspoon sugar

2 tablespoons roughly chopped mint

a pinch of ground cumin

1 Grate the cucumber into a bowl, using a hand grater, add the salt, and mix well. Spread the cucumber out on a dishtowel, gather up the towel, and squeeze out all the excess moisture.

2 Put the cucumber in a bowl and add the yogurt, sugar, mint, and cumin. Mix well and chill until ready to serve.

Variations

MANGO AND TOMATO RAITA

Replace the cucumber with 1 ripe, firm tomato and 1 small mango, both cut into small pieces. Lovely with cold lobster and other seafood.

COCONUT AND GINGER RAITA

Add to the basic raita recipe a 1-inch piece of fresh ginger, peeled and finely grated, and 2 tablespoons unsweetened dried coconut.

CILANTRO AND GREEN CHILE RAITA

Omit the cucumber and replace the mint with fresh cilantro and 2 finely chopped small green chiles. Great with grilled meats, especially burgers.

POMEGRANATE RAITA

Omit the cucumber from the main recipe, then fold in the seeds from 1 fresh pomegranate. A wonderful, refreshing dip in summer.

SPINACH RAITA

Blanch 2½ cups young spinach leaves in boiling water for 30 seconds, then quickly plunge into ice water. Squeeze out excess moisture. Fry in a little oil with ½ garlic clove and 1 teaspoon cumin seeds, let cool, then chop finely. Add a heaping ¾ cup plain yogurt, 2 tablespoons chopped mint, and a squeeze of lemon. Great with legumes, as in the recipe below.

CHICKPEA CAKES WITH SPINACH RAITA

⊕ *I love these vegetarian patties, either with raita as here, or tucked inside hot toasted pita breads. I often serve them atop large, grilled portobello mushrooms—absolutely delicious.*

serves 4

18 ounces cooked dried chickpeas
   (or canned, well drained)

3 cage-free eggs

2 scallions, finely chopped

3 tablespoons tahini (sesame seed paste)

1 small onion, finely chopped

½ garlic clove, crushed

2 tablespoons olive oil

1¼ cups fresh white breadcrumbs

3 tablespoons chopped cilantro

salt and freshly cracked black pepper

¾–1 cup spinach raita (see above), for serving

1 Blitz the chickpeas, eggs, scallions, and tahini in a blender, then transfer to a mixing bowl.

2 Sweat the onions and garlic in half the oil until softened. Add to the chickpea mixture along with the breadcrumbs and cilantro. Season and mix well.

3 Using your hands, form into 8 equal-sized patties, then put them in the fridge to set for up to 1 hour.

4 Heat the remaining oil in a large, nonstick frying pan. Cook the patties, 4 at a time, until golden all over, about 4–5 minutes. Serve immediately with the spinach raita.

CILANTRO CHUTNEY

This basic Indian-style chutney can be made either raw or cooked, and I include both versions here. ⊕ *Either way, it makes a great dipping sauce for serving with grilled lamb cutlets, crispy spicy samosas, or simply with poppadoms.*

for the raw chutney

makes ¾–1 cup

3½ ounces cilantro, stalks included
   (about ½ bunch)
2 hot green chiles, chopped
1-inch piece of fresh ginger, peeled and grated
2 garlic cloves
½ teaspoon ground cumin
juice of ½ lemon
½ teaspoon salt
½ teaspoon sugar
¼ cup coconut milk or plain yogurt

1 Put all the ingredients except for the coconut milk or yogurt in a blender and blitz to a coarse puree.
2 Add the coconut milk or yogurt and blitz again until smooth, then transfer to a jar or covered bowl and refrigerate. The raw chutney will keep in the fridge for 2–3 days.

for the cooked chutney

makes ¾–1 cup

scant ½ cup vegetable oil
2 hot green chiles, chopped
3½ ounces cilantro, stalks included
salt
⅓ cup water
½ teaspoon black mustard seeds
½ teaspoon ground cumin
2 tablespoons urad dal (black lentils)
4 curry leaves

1 Heat half the oil in a pan, add the chiles and cilantro, and fry for 30 seconds. Remove from the heat and let cool.
2 When the mixture is cool, transfer to a small blender along with a little salt and the water, and blitz to a paste.
3 Heat the remaining oil in a pan and add the mustard seeds, cumin, and urad dal. When it begins to splutter, add the curry leaves along with the chile and cilantro mixture and cook for 10–20 seconds, just long enough to infuse the flavors.
4 Transfer to the blender and blitz until smooth. Let cool before serving. The cooked chutney will keep for 2–3 days in a sealed jar in the fridge.

BLATJANG

(dried fruit chutney sauce)

Blatjang is a bit like a chutney, but with a smoother consistency. ⊕ *It is wonderful with cold cuts, but I particularly like it served with cheese, especially washed-rind Époisse, or creamy blue-veined Stilton.*

makes 4 cups

14 ounces mixed dried fruit such as fig, apricot, and pear, soaked in water until softened

½ cup raisins

1 onion, finely chopped

1 hot red chile, finely chopped (or more, according to taste)

2 garlic cloves, crushed

3 cups water

1 tablespoon ground ginger

½ tablespoon ground coriander

½ teaspoon ground cinnamon

3½ tablespoons distilled white vinegar

½ cup soft brown sugar

salt and a pinch of cayenne pepper

1 Cut the dried fruit into small pieces, about ½ inch across.

2 Put all the ingredients in a heavy pan and quickly bring to a boil.

3 Lower the heat and simmer, uncovered, for 45 minutes–1 hour, until the fruits are thick, syrupy, and broken up into a pulp. Add a little more water during the cooking process if the sauce becomes too thick.

SWEET CHILI SAUCE

This Thai sauce has a wonderful, distinctive flavor: it's intensely thick and sweet, with a copious amount of garlic. Bird's-eye (Thai) chiles are fiery little numbers and really add a punch to southern Asian foods. If you can't find them, use the smallest ones available—this generally means the hottest.

makes 1¼ cups

8 bird's-eye (Thai) chiles, half of them pureed in
   a small blender, the rest finely chopped
scant ½ cup hot water
1 heaping cup sugar
scant ½ cup distilled white vinegar
6 large garlic cloves, crushed
1 teaspoon salt
1 tablespoon nam pla (Thai fish sauce)
juice of 1 small lime

1 Put the chiles in a pan, pour in the hot water, and let soften for 20 minutes.
2 Once the chiles have softened, heat them in their soaking water, then add the sugar, vinegar, garlic, and salt, and bring to a boil.
3 Simmer for 12–15 minutes, until syrupy.
4 Stir in the nam pla and lime juice, then let cool at room temperature. Keep the sauce in a tightly sealed jar, stored at room temperature for up to 1 month.

Variation

MANGO KERABU

For a Malaysian-style variation to serve with fried rice as a side dish, add 1 chopped small mango and 2 tablespoons each of chopped cilantro and mint to 4 tablespoons of the finished sweet chili sauce.

PG tip If you want a thicker sauce, "slake" it by stirring 1 teaspoon cornstarch with 1 tablespoon water and adding it to the finished sauce. I love this sauce; I use it like tomato ketchup. Try adding a couple of spoonfuls to mayonnaise with a little grated fresh ginger and serving it with fish and chips —heaven!

TOMATO AND COCONUT SAMBAL

The word sambal is prevalent in the vocabulary of India and many South Asian and Pacific Rim countries. In Sri Lanka, sambals are often a little milder as they include coconut milk, whereas further east they pack a more fiery power. ⊕ *This particular version is served warm and is fantastic with grilled fish, especially on a bed of cinnamon-steamed jasmine rice.*

makes 1½ cups

2 tablespoons vegetable oil
1 shallot, thinly sliced
2 green chiles, finely chopped (or finely sliced if
   you are using a thinner variety of chile)
1-inch piece of fresh ginger, peeled and grated
1 garlic clove, sliced
2 teaspoons mild curry powder
6 curry leaves
7 ounces cherry tomatoes
scant ½ cup thick coconut milk
juice of 2 limes
10 Thai sweet basil leaves
salt

1 Heat the oil in a wok or frying pan and add the shallot, chiles, ginger, and garlic. Cook over a low heat for 4–5 minutes.
2 Add the curry powder, curry leaves, and tomatoes, and cook for 2–3 minutes.
3 Pour in the thick coconut milk and lime juice, and cook for a final 5 minutes.
4 Stir in the basil, season with the salt, and serve.

TOMATO SAMBAL

From neighboring Bali, this is great served with barbecued fish. Add 2 tablespoons finely chopped tomatoes to the basic recipe.

LEMONGRASS AND SHALLOT SAMBAL

Add 4 very finely chopped stalks of lemongrass (outer husk removed) and 2 chopped shallots to the basic recipe.

INDONESIAN SWEET POTATO SOUP

The natural sweetness in sweet potato makes it the perfect vegetable for this Asian-inspired soup, which I first prepared many years ago for an American guest who requested a spicy hot soup flavored with coconut. This is my result—and it was a hit!

SAMBAL OELEK

This Indonesian-inspired chili sauce is to Asian dishes what harissa is to Moroccan: a little spoonful adds a spice kick and enlivens food in seconds.
⊕ *Serve with meat, or add to stir-fries and fried rice. I often add a little to a pizza base and top it with barbecued chicken, for an Asian-style pizza.*

makes ¾–1 cup

2 garlic cloves, crushed

½ teaspoon dried shrimp paste (terasi or blachan)

1 teaspoon salt

4 large red chiles, chopped

1 teaspoon sugar

2 limes, peeled and cut into small pieces

¼ cup hot water

1 tablespoon rice wine vinegar

⅓ cup plus 1 tablespoon nam pla (Thai fish sauce)

2 tablespoons Thai sweet basil leaves

1 Put the garlic, shrimp paste, salt, and chiles in a mortar and pound to a coarse paste with a pestle. (This can be done in a blender if you prefer.)

2 Add the sugar, limes, water, vinegar, and nam pla, and pound (or blend) to a thick paste. Add the sweet basil leaves and pound (or blend) again. Store in a sealed container in the fridge for up to 1 month.

serves 4

4 cups well-flavored chicken stock (see page 9)

4 stalks of lemongrass, outer husks removed, chopped

1 recipe sambal oelek (see left)

⅔ ounce cilantro leaves and stalks, separated

2-inch piece of galangal or fresh ginger, peeled and chopped

2 sweet potatoes, peeled and cut into small chunks

⅔ cup coconut milk

1 tablespoon nam pla (Thai fish sauce)

1 Put the chicken stock, lemongrass, sambal oelek, and cilantro stalks in a pan and bring to a boil. Reduce to a simmer and cook for 10 minutes.

2 Add the galangal or ginger, and the sweet potatoes to the pan and simmer for 15 minutes, or until very soft. Remove from the heat and let cool slightly.

3 Transfer to a blender and blitz until smooth, then strain into a clean pan.

4 Add the coconut milk and nam pla and simmer for 5 minutes. Stir in the cilantro leaves and serve.

ACHIN

(garlic and ginger fish sauce)

The food of Burma reflects the influences of the country's many neighbors, especially the largest, India and China. Indian influences can be seen in the use of tamarind, and Chinese in the abundance of ginger, garlic, and soy sauce. ⊕ *I recently tasted this sauce while visiting the Burmese-Thai border, where it was served with crisp tempura-fried vegetables.*

makes ⅔ cup

2 garlic cloves, chopped

1-inch piece of fresh ginger, peeled and chopped

¼ cup tamarind paste

¼ cup honey

1 teaspoon sugar

1 tablespoon soy sauce

2 teaspoons nam pla (Thai fish sauce)

1 small red pepper, chopped

a pinch each of salt and paprika

1 Pound the garlic and ginger in a mortar (or blender) to a fine paste, then transfer to a bowl.

2 Add the remaining ingredients and stir to form a smooth sauce. It can be kept in a sealed container in the fridge for up to 7 days.

ASIAN GINGER DRESSING

⊕ *A terrific dressing for steamed fish or shellfish, and also great for Asian-style vegetable salads.*

makes ⅔ cup

2 tablespoons nam pla (Thai fish sauce)

2 tablespoons water

2 tablespoons rice wine vinegar

2 tablespoons light soy sauce

2 teaspoons sugar

10 mint leaves

1 shallot, finely chopped

1-inch piece of fresh ginger, peeled and grated

salt and freshly cracked black pepper

1 Mix all the ingredients in a bowl with salt and pepper to taste and let infuse for 1 hour. This sauce will keep only for 1–2 days in the fridge; after that it will lose its freshness of flavor.

THAI CURRY SAUCE

There are some perfectly acceptable prepared red and green pastes on the market, but to my mind they don't compare with those made at home.

Authentic Thai sauces are made by first producing a spice paste, either red, using dried red chiles, or green, using fresh green chiles. The green is hotter and more sour in flavor than the red, but both are delicious.

Knobby-looking galangal, with its almost camphorized scent and flavor, is similar to ginger root, but really does add a different flavor to the sauce. It is available from Asian grocers, but fresh ginger root is an acceptable substitute. The paste will keep perfectly well in a sealed container in the fridge for up to 2 months.

makes about 3 cups
for red curry paste

1 tablespoon coriander seeds
1 tablespoon cumin seeds
10 dried red chiles (or fresh)
1 teaspoon dried shrimp paste (terasi or blachan)
3 shallots, chopped
1-inch piece of fresh galangal or ginger, chopped
3 stalks of lemongrass, outer husks removed, finely chopped
4 kaffir lime leaves, torn
grated zest of 1 lime
2 tablespoons cilantro stalks or leaves, chopped

1 Heat a heavy frying pan over a high heat, add the coriander and cumin seeds, and quickly brown until golden, stirring constantly.
2 Transfer to a mortar or blender, add the remaining ingredients, and pound or blitz to a smooth paste; it may be necessary to scrape down the sides of the blender, if using, during the process.

for the curry sauce

1 tablespoon vegetable oil
14-ounce can unsweetened thick coconut milk
2 tablespoons red or green curry paste (see left and above)
2 x 14-ounce cans unsweetened coconut milk
2 tablespoons nam pla (Thai fish sauce)
4 kaffir lime leaves, torn

1 Heat the oil in a heavy pan, add the thick coconut milk, and cook for 15–20 minutes until it splits (separates).
2 Add the curry paste, cook for 10 minutes, then add the coconut milk, nam pla, and lime leaves, and simmer for 20 minutes. The sauce is now ready for using in the recipe of your choice.

Variations

GREEN CURRY PASTE
Replace the red chiles with the same amount of bird's-eye (Thai) green chiles and proceed in the same way as for red.

LEMONGRASS CURRY PASTE
For a lemongrass curry sauce from neighboring Cambodia, add 6 finely chopped lemongrass stalks, a pinch of ground turmeric and 1 teaspoon dried shrimp paste to a basic green curry sauce as it cooks.

MINTED PEA EGGPLANT AND BEAN CURRY

Pea eggplants are an Asian variety of eggplant and, as their name suggests, are pea-shaped and about the size of a large grape. They are very bitter, and add a tart, astringent flavor to the curry.

serves 4

5 ounces green beans (about 1 cup)

2 tablespoons vegetable or peanut oil

4 green chiles, thinly sliced

2-inch piece of fresh ginger, peeled and
    thinly sliced

8 ounces pea eggplants (see above)

2½ cups Thai green curry sauce (see opposite)

¾ cup shelled fava beans (frozen or fresh)

4 ripe, firm tomatoes, chopped

1 tablespoon tamarind paste

1¾ ounces small fresh mint leaves

steamed jasmine or basmati rice, for serving

1 Blanch the green beans in boiling, salted water for 2–3 minutes, then refresh in cold water and dry them.

2 Heat the oil in a wok over medium heat and add the chiles and ginger. Fry until lightly softened, 2–3 minutes.

3 Add the pea eggplants, then the green curry sauce, and cook for 5 minutes.

4 Add the blanched green beans, fava beans, and tomatoes, and cook for another 5–8 minutes.

5 Stir in the tamarind and the mint leaves, and serve over the steamed rice.

TAMARIND SAUCE

Tamarind, from the pods of the tamarind tree, is a distinctive souring agent. It can be purchased in dried block form (pulp) or as a concentrate or paste.
⊕ *This sauce is great with crispy-fried samosas as a dip, or with other Indian snacks such as bhel poori. It also makes a wonderful glaze for barbecued chicken as it cooks, or for fried fish.*

makes 1¾ cups

5½-ounce block tamarind pulp, chopped

1 small, red bird's-eye (Thai) chile

1-inch piece of fresh ginger, peeled and chopped

¼ cup soft light brown sugar or 2 tablespoons honey

1 tablespoon soy sauce

1 garlic clove, crushed

1 Soak the tamarind pulp in 1¼ cups boiling water for 2 hours, or until soft. (If you are in a hurry, simmer the tamarind in the water in a pan for 20 minutes.)

2 Pour the pulp into a strainer set over a clean pan and push it through, using a wooden spoon.

3 Add the remaining ingredients and ⅔ cup cold water to the pan, then bring to a boil and simmer for 5 minutes.

4 Let cool, adding a little more sugar to taste if necessary. Store in a sealed container in the fridge for up to 4 days, or frozen for up to 3 months.

Variations

ORANGE-TAMARIND SAUCE

Replace the cold water in step 3 with the juice and grated zest of 1 orange; lovely with roast duck.

MINT TAMARIND

Add 2 tablespoons mint sauce (see page 72) to the finished sauce.

TAMARIND KETCHUP

Mix half the sauce with an equal amount of tomato ketchup and add 2 tablespoons chopped cilantro.

INDONESIAN PEANUT SAUCE

Peanut sauces can be found in many Asian and Pacific Rim cuisines, generally served with satays and spring rolls. In Indonesia, they tend to be spicier than further east, with a little curry paste added.

makes 1¾ cups

1 tablespoon vegetable oil

1 shallot, finely chopped

2 garlic cloves, crushed

scant cup coconut milk

2 teaspoons red curry paste (see page 150)

1 teaspoon dried shrimp paste (terasi or blachan; optional)

2 teaspoons sugar

½ cup water

3½ ounces crunchy peanut butter

2 teaspoons kecap manis (Indonesian soy sauce)

a drizzle of hot chili oil (optional), for serving

1 Heat the oil in a heavy pan and add the shallot and garlic. Cook for 4–5 minutes until softened.
2 Add the coconut milk and bring to a boil. Stir in the curry paste, shrimp paste, if using, and sugar.
3 Whisk in the water and peanut butter, reduce the heat, and add the kecap manis. Simmer for 1 minute, then transfer the sauce to a serving dish and serve warm, drizzled with a little chili oil, if using. Kept in the fridge in a sealed container, this sauce will last for 3–4 days.

GADO GADO

The beauty of this Indonesian vegetable salad lies both in its simplicity and the variation of textures in the vegetables. Sometimes it also includes tofu, which is a handy addition for vegetarians. If you have an egg slicer, use it here for thin, even slices.

serves 4

1 tablespoon mango chutney

scant cup Indonesian peanut sauce (see left)

7 ounces baby new potatoes, boiled and cooled

2 small carrots, thinly sliced in rounds and lightly cooked

⅓ cup cooked green beans, cut into small lengths

1 cup bean sprouts

¼ English cucumber, cut in half lengthwise and sliced

2 tomatoes, each cut into 4 slices

salt and freshly cracked black pepper

2 cage-free eggs, hard-boiled, peeled, and thinly sliced

2 tablespoons roughly chopped roasted peanuts

1 In a large bowl, stir the mango chutney into the peanut sauce. Add the potatoes, carrots, beans, bean sprouts, cucumber, and tomatoes, with salt and pepper to taste, and mix well.
2 Put a stainless-steel ring or 3-inch cookie cutter on a plate, then fill it with the salad, pressing it down lightly to compact.
3 Remove the ring or cutter, decorate the top with overlapping egg slices, and sprinkle with peanuts.
4 Repeat the ring/cookie cutter process on 3 more plates and serve at room temperature.

PG tip Many good kitchenware stores sell stainless-steel rings, but otherwise a 14-ounce can opened at both ends makes a perfect mold for use in the kitchen.

THE PACIFIC rim

Clustered around the immense Pacific Ocean, this loose grouping of countries stretches from Vietnam, China, and Japan all the way around to the American West Coast and has great culinary diversity. Japanese sauces tend to be highly concentrated, served in small amounts and designed to set off the flavor of exquisite morsels of food—perhaps a pungent wasabi sauce to go with sashimi, or ponzu, a sour dipping sauce made from soy and yuzu (an oriental citrus fruit), to accompany chilled shellfish—especially good with oysters. In China, too, sauces are light yet emphatic, often based on strong, salty, fermented foods such as soybeans and black beans, with ginger and garlic to refresh the flavor. This lightness of touch also characterises the cooking of the West Coast of America. With its checkered history, this area has absorbed culinary influences from Spain, Mexico, Italy, and the immigrant Chinese population. Healthy foods such as salads and stir-fries reign supreme, and vinaigrettes and marinades often take the place of richer sauces.

ADOBO

Adobo is Spanish for marinade, and I have been lucky enough to taste different types across the globe. They all seem to vary in flavor, but in Mexico, heat is the major factor; in southern Asia they seem to have an acidic flavor too, but chile is always the main ingredient.

Annatto, also known as achiote, which is the tree it comes from, is a reddish-brown seed, which can be bought whole or in powder form. It adds a wonderful orange color, and is used widely as a natural food coloring.

makes 2½ cups

1 tablespoon vegetable oil

4 hot red chiles, roughly chopped

3 garlic cloves, crushed

2 tablespoons tomato paste

⅔ cup white wine vinegar

1 cup chicken stock (see page 8)

1 bay leaf

2 teaspoons crushed coriander seeds

1 teaspoon annatto powder (or seeds)

¼ cup soy sauce

½ teaspoon freshly cracked black peppercorns

1 teaspoon sugar

salt

1 Heat the oil in a frying pan, add the chiles and garlic, and cook over a low heat until the chiles are lightly golden and blistered.

2 Add the tomato paste and cook for another 3–4 minutes.

3 Transfer to a blender and add the remaining ingredients except the salt. Blitz until smooth, then return to the pan and cook over a low heat for 15–20 minutes.

4 Season to taste; the mixture should be slightly sweet and sour in flavor with a hint of saltiness. It will keep for several days in a sealed container in the fridge.

PORK STRIPS IN ADOBO

(for 4 people)

Put 1 pound, 10 ounces boneless belly pork strips, cut into small pieces, in a shallow dish and pour 1¼ cups adobo sauce over them. Cover and let marinate in the fridge for 4 hours. Heat 2 tablespoons vegetable oil in a wok or large frying pan and quickly fry the marinated pork pieces until golden. Add the marinade to the wok, cover, and cook for 5 minutes, stirring occasionally, or until the sauce has reduced slightly. Serve the pork in its sauce with steamed basmati or jasmine rice. You could also make this dish with chicken pieces instead of pork.

CHAR SUI

Whenever I visit London's Soho, I always take time out to visit the Chinese restaurants and, understandably, always buy and consume far too many char sui buns. They are out of this world: pork steamed in fluffy dough and bound inside in this sweet, sticky barbecue sauce. It's great too with barbecued meat, such as pork or chicken.

makes 1¼ cups

3½ tablespoons dry sherry

scant ½ cup hoisin sauce (see page 160 for homemade)

3½ tablespoons light soy sauce

¼ cup sugar

4 garlic cloves

1 tablespoon black bean paste

½ teaspoon Chinese five-spice powder

2 shallots, finely chopped

salt

1 Put all the ingredients, except the salt, in a pan and slowly bring to a boil.

2 Lower the heat and simmer, uncovered, for 10–12 minutes, or until thick. Add salt to taste and let cool completely before using.

CHINESE PEANUT SAUCE

Less spicy than the Indonesian version of the sauce (see page 153). ⊕ *This is very good served with spring rolls or satays.*

makes 1¼ cups

½ cup chicken stock (see page 8)

¼ cup smooth or crunchy peanut butter, or ¾ cup roasted peanuts

2 tablespoons light soy sauce

2 garlic cloves, crushed

1 tablespoon rice wine vinegar

3 teaspoons sugar

¼ teaspoon chili powder

2 tablespoons chopped cilantro leaves

1 Put the stock in a pan and bring to a boil. Add the peanut butter or peanuts, soy sauce, and garlic, and simmer for 2–3 minutes.

2 Transfer to a blender and add the vinegar, sugar, chili powder, and cilantro.

3 Blitz to a coarse sauce-like consistency.

JAPANESE ROASTED SESAME SEED SAUCE

An extremely versatile sauce, but I love it best with fried rice; it adds an instant flavor burst. ⊕ *It also makes an excellent dipping sauce and goes very well with most vegetables, especially green beans or broccoli.*

makes ¾–1 cup

4 ounces Japanese white sesame seeds
   (see tip below)
1 tablespoon sesame oil
1 tablespoon vegetable oil
⅔ cup shoyu (Japanese soy sauce)
2 tablespoons mirin (Japanese sweet rice wine)
1 tablespoon brown sugar
½ teaspoon dashi (see page 9) mixed with a
   scant ½ cup warm water

1 Heat a dry frying pan or wok over a high heat and, when it is almost smoking, add the sesame seeds and fry until golden, keeping the seeds moving to prevent them burning. Transfer to a mortar.
2 Add both oils and crush the seeds to a paste with a pestle.
3 Stir in the shoyu, mirin, sugar, and dashi and water mixture, transfer to a bowl, and refrigerate until needed. It is best eaten within 1–2 days.

PG tip Japanese sesame seeds, known as gomaiso, are plumper than normal sesame seeds, and have a nuttier, more complex flavor. They are available from Asian stores, but if you can't find them, ordinary ones will do here.

SICHUAN SAUCE

The Sichuan region of China is noted for its gastronomy, and for its fiery dishes and sauces in particular. This classic chili sauce is wonderful with stir-fried noodles and vegetables, or sprinkled over steamed fragrant rice. There are recipes for tomato ketchup and hoisin sauce elsewhere in this book, if you want to make your own, but bottled will be fine here.

makes 1¾ cups

2 tablespoons tomato ketchup (see page 167
   for homemade)
2 tablespoons hoisin sauce (see page 160 for
   homemade)
2 tablespoons black bean sauce
1 tablespoon plum sauce
2 tablespoons Shaoxing wine or dry sherry
2 teaspoons Chinese black vinegar
2 teaspoons chili paste
2 tablespoons light soy sauce
2 tablespoons peanut oil
2 garlic cloves, crushed
2-inch piece of fresh ginger, peeled and grated
⅔ cup chicken stock (see page 8)
2 teaspoons sesame oil

1 Put the ketchup, hoisin sauce, black bean sauce, plum sauce, wine or sherry, vinegar, chili paste, and soy sauce in a bowl.
2 Heat the peanut oil in a wok or frying pan and add the garlic and ginger. Cook for 1 minute, then add the mixture in the bowl to the pan, along with the stock. Cook for 4–5 minutes, remove from the heat, add the sesame oil, and serve.

HOISIN SAUCE

Also known as Peking sauce, hoisin sauce is a thick, reddish-brown Chinese dipping sauce with a flavor best described as a blend of sweet, salty, and spicy overtones. Made from fermented soybeans, sugar, garlic, and chile, it is commonly served with barbecued meats, especially fatty ones, and Peking duck. It also forms the base of many other Chinese-style sauces.

It is possible to buy ready-made hoisin, but here is my version, given to me by a Chinese chef friend.

makes 1¼ cups

2 garlic cloves

1 red chile, seeded and finely chopped

4 ounces black bean paste

4 teaspoons sesame oil

4 teaspoons rice wine vinegar or distilled
white vinegar

⅓ cup dark soy sauce

3 tablespoons molasses or honey

1 Put the garlic in a mortar and, using a pestle, crush it to a fine paste.

2 Add the chile and crush again to a paste.

3 Add the black bean paste, sesame oil, and vinegar, then stir in the soy sauce.

4 Heat the molasses or honey in a small pan and stir it into the paste. You may need to add more soy sauce or bean paste, depending on your preferred flavor balance.

ROAST DUCK PEKING STYLE

Traditionally, Peking-style duck takes an age to prepare: first the blanching of the ducks in boiling water to break down the fat, then drying the skins by hanging them in an airy place. The sight of some 50 ducks hanging on hooks around the perimeter of a Chinese kitchen is one of my favorite memories from my time in Asia. But don't panic—my adaptation of the dish here is far quicker and just as tasty.

serves 4

1 duck, about 3¾ pounds

¼ cup hoisin sauce (see left)

1 teaspoon peeled and grated fresh ginger

½ teaspoon Chinese five-spice powder

2 tablespoons honey

1 tablespoon light soy sauce

1 tablespoon sweet sherry

1 garlic clove, crushed

1 Blanch the whole duck in a large pot of boiling water (or hold the duck over the sink and very carefully pour boiling water over it, rotating it so that the skin is scalded). Dry well with a cloth.

2 Preheat the oven to 400°F.

3 Put all the remaining ingredients in a pan and bring slowly to a bowl. Remove from the heat and brush liberally over the duck, inside and out.

4 Place the duck on a rack in a roasting pan and roast for 1½ hours, until caramelized and sticky, with a crisp skin. Turn the oven down to 350°F and cook for another 40 minutes.

5 Remove the duck from the oven and let cool before cutting into pieces. Serve with sautéed shiitake mushrooms, steamed Chinese greens, and some extra hoisin sauce mixed with a little hot water.

PG tip If you don't have a roasting rack, a cake cooling rack is fine.

ROAST DUCK
PEKING STYLE

If you want to strive for maximum authenticity, by all means try hanging the blanched and dried duck at room temperature for 5 hours before roasting— the skin should crisp up really nicely.

JAPANESE MUSTARD SAUCE

⊕ *Serve this hot sauce smeared on a thick, juicy steak or pork chop—it's just marvelous.*

makes about ⅔ cup

2 garlic cloves, crushed

1 tablespoon pickled ginger

1 teaspoon toasted sesame seeds

½ teaspoon wasabi paste (Japanese horseradish)

2 tablespoons Dijon mustard

1 teaspoon mirin (Japanese sweet rice wine)

1 teaspoon soy sauce

1 Put the garlic, ginger, sesame seeds, and wasabi paste in a mortar and crush to a fine paste with a pestle.

2 Transfer to a bowl and stir in the mustard.

3 Add the mirin and soy sauce and mix well.

TERIYAKI

The name teriyaki derives from *teri*, meaning to give shine and lustre, and *yaki*, which refers to the grilling method of cooking. Traditionally the cooked ingredient is dipped in or brushed with sauce several times before and during cooking. The inclusion of molasses is not strictly traditional but I think it gives a really unctuous taste and shine. In Japan a little grated fresh ginger is also sometimes added.

You can buy teriyaki in bottles, but for me it just does not compare with the homemade variety, which is so easy to prepare. ⊕ *It goes wonderfully with fish, meat, poultry, and vegetables—as a marinade, cooking sauce, or glaze.*

makes 1¼ cups

½ cup shoyu (Japanese soy sauce)

2 tablespoons mirin (Japanese sweet rice wine)

1 tablespoon brown sugar

3 tablespoons black treacle or molasses

1 Put all the ingredients in a small pan and bring gently to a boil. Simmer for 10 minutes until syrupy, then let cool.

Variations

WASABI GINGER TERIYAKI

Add 1 teaspoon peeled and grated fresh ginger to the basic recipe and whisk ¼ teaspoon wasabi paste into the cooled, finished sauce.

BARBECUE TERIYAKI

Whisk 1 teaspoon Dijon mustard and the grated zest and juice of 1 small orange into the cooled, finished sauce.

BARBECUE TERIYAKI-GLAZED SCALLOPS (for 4 people)

Place 12 medium-large, cleaned fresh scallops, out of their shells, in a shallow dish, then pour ⅔ cup of the teriyaki sauce over them. Cover and let marinate for 1 hour in the fridge.

Cook quickly on a hot barbecue or grill pan for 1 minute on each side, brushing regularly with the marinade. At the same time, heat another scant ½ cup teriyaki sauce (don't use the marinade, as it has been in contact with raw fish). Serve the grilled scallops immediately, with some grilled baby leeks and the hot teriyaki.

CHIBA SAUCE

(wasabi mayonnaise)

Chiba sauce is a dipping sauce from Japan, ideal to serve with tempura, delicate herb leaves such as shiso (also known as perilla), vegetables, seafood, or meat, or just as a spicy dip for french fries or chips. If you are not familiar with wasabi, take care as it packs a punch—you might prefer to adjust the quantity according to your taste.

makes ¾–1 cup

½ teaspoon wasabi paste (Japanese horseradish)

⅔ cup homemade mayonnaise (see page 30)

2 tablespoons whipping cream

2 teaspoons shoyu (Japanese soy sauce)

1 Mix all the ingredients together in a bowl. The sauce will keep in the fridge in a sealed container for 3–4 days.

SEAFOOD IN NORI TEMPURA BATTER WITH CHIBA SAUCE

serves 4

6 cleaned scallops, cut in half horizontally

12 large oysters, out of their shells

8 large tiger shrimp, peeled

vegetable oil, for deep-frying

scant ½ cup chiba sauce (see left) and lime wedges, for serving

for the batter

2½ tablespoons flour

¾ cup cornstarch

1 sheet of nori seaweed, finely chopped

salt

¾ cup ice-cold water

1 large cage-free egg white, lightly beaten

1 Make the batter by mixing the flour, cornstarch, and chopped seaweed in a bowl with a little salt.
2 Add the ice-cold water and beaten egg white and stir until just mixed: the batter should still be lumpy.
3 Heat the oil to 350°F in a deep-fryer or deep pan. Season the seafood and dip each piece into the batter, then drop into the hot oil. You will have to do this in two batches, so season and batter only half the seafood at this stage.
4 Deep-fry for 1 minute until golden and crispy. Remove with a slotted spoon onto paper towels and keep warm while you batter and cook the rest.
5 Divide the seafood equally between 4 serving plates and serve with the chiba sauce and lime wedges.

SWEET AND SOUR SAUCE

One of the most loved sauces in the Chinese repertoire. ⊕ *Serve it with crispy-fried pork or chicken, or as a dipping sauce—wonderful!*

makes 1¾ cups

⅔ cup rice wine vinegar

2 tablespoons sake or dry sherry

⅓ cup soft brown sugar

2 tablespoons tomato ketchup (see page 167 for homemade)

2 teaspoons light soy sauce

4 teaspoons cornstarch, mixed with

    4 teaspoons water

1 Put the vinegar, sake or sherry, sugar, ketchup, and soy sauce in a pan and bring to a boil. Reduce the heat and simmer for 4–5 minutes.

2 Stir the cornstarch and water mixture into the simmering sauce and cook for another 1 minute.

Variation

HUNAN SAUCE

This is best described as a spicy variation of sweet and sour sauce. Just add 2 tablespoons sweet chili sauce or sambal oelek (see page 148) and a 1-inch piece of fresh ginger, peeled and grated, to the basic recipe. A real treat cooked with chicken or shrimp.

PG tip Sometimes cubed fresh pineapple, sliced pepper, sliced scallions, or sliced carrots are added and cooked in the sauce before thickening.

CHINESE BLACK BEAN SAUCE

makes 1¼ cups

2 tablespoons sesame oil

1 tablespoon peanut oil

2 garlic cloves, crushed

1-inch piece of fresh ginger, peeled and finely chopped

a heaping ⅓ cup Chinese black beans, coarsely chopped

⅔ cup well-flavored chicken stock (see page 8)

3 tablespoons dark soy sauce

1 tablespoon mirin (Japanese sweet rice wine)

1 teaspoon sugar

1 teaspoon cornstarch, mixed with

    1 teaspoon water

1 Heat both oils in a wok over a high heat. Add the garlic, ginger, and black beans and fry for 1 minute.

2 Add the stock, soy sauce, mirin, and sugar, and bring to a boil.

3 Simmer for 2 minutes, then stir in the cornstarch and water mixture until the sauce thickens.

STIR-FRIED BEEF WITH BLACK BEAN SAUCE (for 4 people)

Cut 1 pound, 10 ounces beef tenderloin into thin strips. Heat a little peanut oil in a wok or frying pan and add the beef in batches to ensure the wok or pan stays hot during the cooking. Cook for 1–2 minutes until sealed, then remove each batch to a plate and keep it warm while you cook the remaining beef. After the last batch, return all the beef to the wok with ¾–1 cup black bean sauce (see above) and cook for 2 minutes. Serve the beef in the sauce, with steamed broccoli and rice.

CLASSIC SHRIMP COCKTAIL SAUCE

This hot and zingy little cocktail sauce is a favorite throughout America. ⊕ *Serve it as a dip for shrimp and other seafood.*

makes 1¼ cups

scant cup tomato ketchup (see right for homemade)

2 tablespoons grated fresh horseradish

1 garlic clove, crushed

juice of 1 lemon

3 drops of Tabasco sauce

salt and freshly cracked black pepper

1 Mix all the ingredients in a bowl with salt and pepper to taste. The sauce will keep in the fridge for about 1 week, but will lose its freshness after a couple of days.

Variation

JAPANESE-STYLE COCKTAIL SAUCE

Grate a 2-inch piece of peeled fresh ginger and add to the basic recipe, along with 1 tablespoon shoyu (Japanese soy sauce).

CLASSIC TOMATO KETCHUP

Ketchup first appeared in American cookbooks during the early 19th century, but it was as a general term for a sauce made of mushrooms, walnuts, or fruits. Summer is the ideal time to make tomato ketchup, when the best, extremely ripe and well-flavored tomatoes are available.

makes 1 quart

2¼ pounds very ripe, flavorful tomatoes, quartered

1 tablespoon tomato paste

11 ounces onions, chopped

11 ounces cooking apples, peeled, cored, and chopped

4 cups distilled white vinegar or cider vinegar

2¼ tablespoons mustard seeds

½ teaspoon dried red pepper flakes

½ small stick of cinnamon

1 teaspoon ground mace

1 teaspoon black peppercorns

1 teaspoon sea salt or kosher salt

1¼ cups brown sugar

1 Put the tomatoes, tomato paste, onions, and apples in a heavy preserving pan with half the vinegar, and all the spices and the salt.

2 Bring the mixture to a boil, then simmer for 1¾–2 hours, stirring occasionally, until well reduced.

3 Strain the hot mixture through a coarse strainer into a clean preserving pan, discarding any solids.

4 Add the remaining vinegar, and the sugar, then stir the mixture over a low heat until the sugar has dissolved.

5 Bring to a boil and simmer until thick and syrupy. Remove from the heat and let cool.

6 If you want to store it, once the ketchup is cold, pour it into clean, warmed, sterilized jars and keep on a cool shelf. Alternatively, it will keep for up to a month in a covered container in the fridge.

SMOKY MUSTARD BARBECUE SAUCE

Make this a few days before you need it, for the flavors to develop. ⊕ *Use it to baste chicken pieces or pork spare ribs just before they have finished cooking—utterly delicious. My other tip is to spread it lavishly over a rare minute steak, slapped between crusty French bread.*

makes 1¼ cups

2 tablespoons vegetable oil

1 onion, finely chopped

1 garlic clove, crushed

juice of 1 lemon

½ cup soft brown sugar or ⅓ cup honey

¼ cup red wine vinegar

⅔ cup tomato ketchup

   (see page 167 for homemade)

2 tablespoons Worcestershire sauce

1 tablespoon smoked paprika

⅓ cup Mexican-style hot chili sauce or

   ½ teaspoon Tabasco

1 teaspoon Dijon mustard

salt and freshly cracked black pepper

1 Heat the oil in a frying pan and add the onion and garlic. Cook for 5 minutes until soft and lightly browned.

2 Add the remaining ingredients, except the salt and pepper, and simmer for 8–10 minutes. Add salt and pepper to taste and serve.

BULGOGI SAUCE

(Korean barbecue sauce)

⊕ *This sesame-flavored sauce, whose name literally translates as "fire meat," can be used as a marinade as well as a sauce to serve alongside barbecued meat and poultry.*

makes ¾–1 cup

1 garlic clove, crushed

1 teaspoon toasted sesame seeds

½ teaspoon coarse salt

2 teaspoons sugar

2 tablespoons soy sauce

2 teaspoons toasted sesame oil

2 tablespoons water

2 tablespoons rice wine or dry sherry

3 scallions, finely chopped

1 tablespoon hot chili sauce or sambal oelek

   (see page 148)

1 Put the garlic, sesame seeds, salt, and sugar in a mortar and crush to a fine paste with a pestle.

2 Add the remaining ingredients and mix well. The sauce will keep well for 2–3 days in a sealed container in the fridge.

CITRUS PONZU

(lime and ginger dressing)

Ponzu is a traditional dipping sauce or light dressing made from soy and citrus juice. It can be purchased ready-made from Japanese stores, but generally lacks the punch of any freshly made version. Yuzu is a Japanese citrus fruit, often difficult to obtain, but lime is the closest substitute. ⊕ *Fantastic as a marinade for scallops or fresh oysters.*

makes ⅔ cup

2 tablespoons fresh yuzu or lime juice

2 teaspoons Japanese rice wine vinegar

1 tablespoon light soy sauce

2 teaspoons mirin (Japanese sweet rice wine)

1 tablespoon sake

1 teaspoon sugar

2-inch piece of kombu (kelp seaweed)

1-inch piece of fresh ginger, peeled and finely
    grated

½ teaspoon finely grated lime zest, blanched

1 Put all the ingredients, except for the lime zest, in a non-reactive bowl and stir until the sugar has completely dissolved.

2 Cover the bowl with plastic wrap and refrigerate for 24 hours, for the flavors to meld.

3 When ready to serve, remove the kombu and add the blanched lime zest.

JAPANESE SALAD DRESSINGS

You may not immediately think of Japan as a country of salad-lovers, but in fact in this modern world salad forms an integral part of everyday life there, especially among the younger generation. Here are three of the most common Japanese dressings. All are best served immediately, but they can be kept in the fridge for one day.

CREAMY SESAME DRESSING

⊕ *Especially good with salad greens, for a basic green salad.*

makes ⅔ cup

2 tablespoons ground Japanese white sesame seeds (see tip on page 159)
1 teaspoon rice wine vinegar
2 tablespoons vegetable oil
1 teaspoon sugar
1 teaspoon soy sauce
2 tablespoons mayonnaise (see page 30)
1 shallot or small onion, finely chopped

1 Put all the ingredients in a bowl and whisk until amalgamated.

YUZU DRESSING

⊕ *Wonderfully fragrant and refreshing, and great with seafood.*

makes ⅔ cup

¼ cup yuzu juice, fresh or bottled
1 tablespoon shoyu (Japanese soy sauce)
1 teaspoon sugar
⅓ cup vegetable or peanut oil

1 Mix all the ingredients in a bowl.

WASABI AND GINGER DRESSING

⊕ *Great with fish and shellfish, especially crab and oysters.*

makes ⅔ cup

1 teaspoon shoyu (Japanese soy sauce)
2 tablespoons rice wine vinegar
1 tablespoon sugar
½ teaspoon sesame oil
¼ cup vegetable oil
½ teaspoon wasabi paste (Japanese horseradish)
1-inch piece of fresh ginger, peeled and grated

1 Put the shoyu and vinegar in a bowl. Add the sugar and whisk well to mix.
2 Add the remaining ingredients and mix well.

CRAB, RADISH, AND SEAWEED SALAD

Not only a wonderful salad, but extremely healthy and nutritious.

serves 4

4 ounces wakame seaweed, soaked in warm water for 2 hours, then drained
1¾ ounces hijiki seaweed, soaked in warm water for 10 minutes, then drained
6 red radishes, thinly sliced
½ cup daikon radish (Japanese white radish), peeled and thinly sliced
⅔ cup fresh crabmeat
2 tablespoons pickled pink ginger
⅔ cup wasabi and ginger dressing (see above)
1 teaspoon toasted black sesame seeds, for serving

1 Put the drained seaweeds, radishes, daikon, crabmeat, and ginger in a bowl.
2 Add the wasabi and ginger dressing, toss well, and serve on individual plates, sprinkled with the sesame seeds.

EAST meets west

"Fusion" is a relatively new term, applied to a revolution that started in America in the late 1970s but has now been embraced in many parts of the world. Essentially it describes a style of cooking in which chefs experiment with techniques, ingredients, and presentations from diverse culinary traditions, creating new, cross-cultural dishes. When it is done well, the results can be utterly inspired, but it has to be informed by a careful understanding of how flavors work together.

If you are bold enough to experiment with this culinary exchange, it is a very liberating way to cook. This chapter helps you discover the pleasures of adding chile to a traditional French béarnaise sauce, Asian flavorings to an Italian pesto, and Japanese wasabi paste to a balsamic dressing. To some this might seem like heresy, but no one can deny that it opens up a world of exciting possibilities.

ASIAN VIERGE SAUCE

In this light, classic French sauce, traditionally based on olive oil, lemon juice, tomatoes, and herbs, the spicy sambal, ginger, and cumin add an exotic, lively kick. ⊕ *Wonderful with char-grilled chicken.*

makes ¾–1 cup

⅓ cup olive oil

2 garlic cloves, crushed

½ teaspoon cumin seeds, lightly toasted

1-inch piece of fresh ginger, peeled and finely
    grated

4 tomatoes, peeled, seeded and chopped

1 teaspoon sambal oelek (see page 148)

2 tablespoons lemon juice

1 tablespoon chopped flat-leaf parsley

1 tablespoon chopped mint

salt and freshly cracked black pepper

1 Put the olive oil in a pan with the garlic, cumin seeds, and ginger, and heat gently for 1 minute over a low heat.

2 Add the tomatoes and cook for 3–4 minutes until they soften.

3 Add the sambal oelek, lemon juice, parsley, and mint. Season to taste and serve.

E A S T meets west

CHILI TARTARE

This is PG's take on a classic mayonnaise-based sauce, with a little heat added to the traditional version. ⊕ *Serve as you would for usual tartare, with fried fish and chips, or with seafood.*

makes 1¼ cups

⅔ cup mayonnaise (see page 30)

3 tablespoons chopped sweet dill pickles

1 small red onion, finely chopped

2 scallions, finely chopped

1 teaspoon superfine capers, rinsed and coarsely
   chopped

2 tablespoons chopped cilantro leaves

½ teaspoon Tabasco sauce, or 1 green chile,
   finely chopped

1 tablespoon sesame oil

salt and freshly cracked black pepper

grated zest and juice of ½ lemon

1 Put the mayonnaise in a non-reactive bowl. Add the remaining ingredients, except the lemon zest and juice, then cover and refrigerate for at least 1 hour.

2 Add the lemon zest and juice, and adjust the seasoning. The sauce will keep, in a sealed container, for up to 2 days in the fridge.

BALSAMIC WASABI DRESSING

I'm a great lover of Japanese eating, especially sushi, which I think I could quite happily live on! The balance of salty and hot Japanese ingredients is masterly. This Japanese-Italian alliance is basically a vinaigrette with Japanese overtones. ⊕ *Use it as you would a classic vinaigrette, to dress greens and salads, or as I like it, drizzled over a carpaccio of tuna, squid, or octopus.*

makes ⅔ cup

½ teaspoon wasabi paste (Japanese horseradish)

1 teaspoon tamari (Japanese soy sauce)

1 teaspoon sugar

1 tablespoon balsamic vinegar

1 tablespoon rice wine vinegar

1 teaspoon sesame oil

⅓ cup olive oil

1 Put the wasabi and tamari in a bowl, then add the sugar and both vinegars and whisk well.

2 Whisk in the sesame oil, then the olive oil, and cover and chill until needed.

PG tip Tamari is a complex, dark, and richly flavored soy sauce made entirely from soybeans, with no wheat. Shoyu is a lighter Japanese soy sauce, made from half soybeans and half wheat. Tamari is especially good for the growing numbers of people adopting a wheat-free diet.

MY TUNA CARPACCIO

It goes without saying that you need the freshest possible tuna for this recipe.

serves 4

14-ounce piece of tuna loin fillet
2 tablespoons extra virgin olive oil
⅓ cup balsamic wasabi dressing (see page 179)
a little coarsely cracked black pepper
arugula leaves, sliced avocado, and orange segments (optional), for serving

1 Wrap the piece of tuna in plastic wrap and roll into a cylindrical shape, twisting the ends of the plastic to create a sausage effect. Transfer to the freezer for 2–3 hours or until firm but not completely frozen through.

2 Remove from the freezer and place on a cutting board. Cut across in very thin slices, using a long-bladed, very sharp knife.

3 Arrange the slices delicately over 4 individual serving plates, covering the complete area.

4 Brush the slices with a little olive oil, then drizzle over the wasabi balsamic dressing over it and sprinkle with a little cracked black pepper.

5 Decorate the middle of each plate with arugula, avocado, and orange segments, if using. Serve with a little crisp, fresh bread.

Other quick-and-easy
East-meets-West sauce derivatives

SOUTHWEST BÉARNAISE

Add 2 seeded, finely chopped red chiles to the finished béarnaise (see page 24). Great with grilled steak or grilled meaty white fish, such as monkfish.

CHINESE ROUILLE SAUCE

To add a little Oriental charm to a seafood stew or fish soup, replace the chile in the rouille recipe (see page 33) with 2 tablespoons hot chili sauce (sambal oelek, see page 148) and add 1 teaspoon light soy sauce.

PICKLED GINGER AND TOMATO SALSA

For a Japanese-inspired salsa, chop some vine tomatoes, mixed peppers, and garlic, and put in a bowl. Add a little soy sauce, rice wine vinegar, sugar, and a little hot chili sauce (sambal oelek, see page 148) to balance the flavors. Finally, add some finely chopped pickled ginger and chopped cilantro. Lovely added to a cold noodle salad or with cold seafood.

TAMARIND-MINT PESTO

Replace the basil in the basic pesto recipe (see page 77) with mint leaves and add a 1-inch piece of fresh ginger, peeled and grated, and 1 teaspoon tamarind paste. Proceed as for the basic recipe. Lovely with grilled fish, grilled lamb, or seafood.

THAI PESTO

Replace the basil in the basic pesto recipe (see page 77) with a 50/50 mixture of cilantro and Thai basil leaves, then add 1 finely chopped red chile and 2 tablespoons sesame oil. Fantastic for pouring over grilled mussels or other seafood such as grilled calamari, shrimp, or clams.

TOMATO MISO SAUCE

Follow the recipe for the classic French-style tomato sauce (see page 58), but after adding the tomato paste, add 2 tablespoons red miso paste, 1 tablespoon soy sauce, and 1 tablespoon mirin (Japanese sweet rice wine). I love this with grilled salmon and stir-fried Asian greens.

THAI STEAK SAUCE

The beauty of this sauce is that it has a dual purpose: it doubles up as a basting sauce for steak, brushed on as it cooks, and an accompaniment for the finished dish. ⊕ *Enjoy it with steak or chicken; it will soon become a favorite.*

makes ⅔ cup

2 tablespoons tamarind paste

¼ cup water

1 tablespoon nam pla (Thai fish sauce)

2 tablespoons palm sugar or soft brown sugar

2 garlic cloves, crushed

¼ cup tomato ketchup
   (see page 167 for homemade)

2 tablespoons sweet chili sauce (see page 146)

1 tablespoon kecap manis (Indonesian soy sauce)

1 Put the tamarind paste and water in a pan and bring to a boil.

2 Add the remaining ingredients and cook for 2 minutes. Remove from the heat and let cool.

JAPANESE SALSA VERDE

Italian salsa verde is one of my favorite sauces. It has everything: piquancy, freshness, and a touch of pungency. In this version, a little Japanese horseradish and peppery mizuna leaves add a Far-Eastern touch to a classic sauce. ⊕ *I love it with salt-grilled mackerel fillets and sliced, hot new potatoes (see below).*

makes ¾–1 cup

1 teaspoon wasabi paste (Japanese horseradish)

⅔ cup olive oil

1 ounce flat-leaf parsley

½ ounce mizuna or arugula leaves (about 1 handful)

¼ cup superfine capers, rinsed

1 tablespoon nam pla (Thai fish sauce)

2 garlic cloves, crushed

juice of 1 lemon

1 Put the wasabi paste in a bowl and slowly whisk in the olive oil.

2 Transfer to a blender, add the remaining ingredients, and blitz to a coarse puree.

BROILED MACKEREL WITH JAPANESE SALSA VERDE

(for 4 people)

Slash the skin of 8 cleaned and trimmed mackerel fillets and season liberally with coarse salt and a little pepper. Place on an oiled baking sheet under a very hot broiler for 3–4 minutes on each side, until cooked. Slice 8 ounces cooked new potatoes and, while they are still hot, mix with 1 thinly sliced red onion, 7 ounces sliced small vine tomatoes (2–3 small tomatoes), and the juice of ½ lemon. Divide this mixture between 4 serving plates and top each with 2 cooked mackerel fillets. Drizzle with ⅓ cup Japanese salsa verde and serve.

SPICY MANGO AÏOLI

You can add all sorts of ingredients to a basic aïoli, and this is just one version using Indian flavorings.

⊕ *It goes particularly well as a spread in a chicken sandwich or with smoked salmon and bacon—a tasty combination. Also great with grilled salmon or lamb chops.*

makes ⅔ cup

2 teaspoons vegetable oil

¼ teaspoon asafetida powder

¼ teaspoon black mustard seeds

4 curry leaves

2 tablespoons finely chopped mango chutney

1 small hot red chile, finely chopped

salt

⅓ cup aïoli (see page 33)

1 Heat the oil in a frying pan over medium heat and sprinkle in the asafetida, mustard seeds, and curry leaves. Fry briefly, until the seeds pop.

2 Add the chutney, chile, and a little salt, then cover and cook for 2 minutes to heat the mixture through. Remove from the heat and set aside to cool.

3 When the mixture is cold, add it to the aïoli; the sauce should be quite hot, creamy, and pleasantly sweet.

THE ULTIMATE CHICKEN SANDWICH

A great sandwich—full of flavor and extremely filling!

serves 4

4 boneless, skinless chicken breasts,
    about 5½ ounces each

2 teaspoons tandoori spice paste

olive oil

8 strips of bacon

4 hamburger buns, sliced in half

2 firm but ripe plum tomatoes, cut into thick slices

leaves of 1 crispy romaine lettuce

4 slices of Emmenthal cheese

⅓ cup spicy mango aïoli (see left)

1 Place the chicken breasts, one at a time, between 2 sheets of plastic wrap and, using a kitchen mallet or rolling pin, pound to an even thickness of about ⅝ inch. Brush the chicken breasts all over with the tandoori spice paste.

2 Heat a grill pan until very hot. Brush it with olive oil and add the chicken breasts. Cook for 2–3 minutes on each side or until cooked through.

3 At the same time, if there is room in the pan, cook the bacon until nice and crispy. Otherwise, remove the chicken and keep it warm while you cook the bacon.

4 Meanwhile, preheat the broiler to hot. Toast the open hamburger buns until golden, then, on the bottom half, place the sliced tomatoes, lettuce, and cooked chicken breast.

5 Cover each chicken breast with 2 strips of the cooked bacon and a slice of cheese, and place briefly under the broiler to melt the cheese.

6 Top with a good spoonful of spicy mango aïoli. Place the top half of the hamburger bun over that, and lightly press down.

YOGURT CHILE SAUCE

A wonderfully refreshing, cool sauce based on the idea of a zippy European cocktail sauce, encompassing many cultural twists and turns. ⊕ *Delicious for binding fresh crabmeat or shrimp.*

makes ⅔ cup

½ onion, finely grated

1-inch piece of fresh ginger, peeled and grated

1 red jalapeño chile, seeded and finely chopped

¼ teaspoon ground turmeric

½ teaspoon sugar

⅓ cup tomato ketchup (see page 167
   for homemade)

1 teaspoon sambal oelek (see page 148), or to taste

3 tablespoons thick plain yogurt

1 tablespoon chopped cilantro leaves

salt and freshly cracked black pepper

1 Put the grated onion and ginger in a bowl, then stir in the remaining ingredients. Season to taste and serve.

MEXICO·VIA·MUMBAI SALSA

I came upon this Asian-style salsa quite by accident one day while preparing an Indian-themed dinner at home for friends. My wife had forgotten to pick up some yogurt for a raita dressing for my appetizer. After raiding the fridge, I improvised with the ingredients I could find, and came up with this Indian-inspired salsa instead. It went down rather well, so I am happy to include it in this section of the book. ⊕ *Serve with Indian-style meats such as kabobs or tandoori chicken, or with grilled fish or seafood.*

makes 1¼ cups

1-inch piece of fresh ginger, peeled and finely
   grated

8 ounces ripe but firm plum tomatoes, chopped
   into small pieces

2½ ounces cucumber, seeded and chopped into
   small pieces

1 red onion, chopped

2 garlic cloves, crushed

2 tablespoons balsamic or rice wine vinegar

juice of 2 large limes

½ teaspoon ground cumin

2 tablespoons chopped cilantro leaves

1 tablespoon chopped mint

1 tablespoon tamarind paste (see tip on page 187)

salt

1 Combine all the ingredients except the salt in a bowl, cover, and leave at room temperature for 1 hour for the flavors to meld.

2 Add salt to taste before serving.

PG tip

MEXICO·VIA·MUMBAI SALSA

Tamarind paste, a traditional element of Asian cuisine, contributes a gently sour flavor with an undercurrent of tropical fruits. Tamarind can occasionally be found as fresh pods, but is more readily available in either compressed dried blocks or as a smooth puree-like paste in jars.

SOY KAFFIR BUTTER SAUCE

Kaffir lime is native to Southeast Asia, where cooks traditionally use the zest and leaves, generally in sauces, or simmered in soups and curries. Ordinary lime zest can be substituted if you can't find kaffir leaves. ⊕ *Any shellfish or grilled fish would be wonderful with this sweet, salty, and sour butter sauce, made using French techniques.*

makes ¾–1 cup

3½ tablespoons unsalted butter, chilled
2 shallots, sliced
⅝-inch piece of fresh ginger, peeled and sliced
3½ tablespoons distilled white vinegar
scant ½ cup chicken stock (see page 8)
3 tablespoons kecap manis (Indonesian soy sauce)
scant ½ cup heavy cream
2 kaffir lime leaves
4 mint leaves
4 Thai sweet basil leaves

1 Heat 1 tablespoon of the butter in a pan, add the shallots and ginger, and cook for 2–3 minutes until lightly softened.

2 Add the vinegar and boil to reduce the liquid by half.

3 Add the stock, kecap manis, and cream, and bring to a boil.

4 Lower the heat and add the lime leaves, mint, and basil leaves, then simmer for 5 minutes.

5 Remove from the heat, whisk in the remaining butter, then strain through a fine strainer before serving hot.

GRILLED LOBSTER WITH SOY KAFFIR BUTTER

serves 4

2 live lobsters, about 1½ pounds each
a little salt and freshly cracked black pepper
1¾ tablespoons unsalted butter, melted
1 tablespoon nam pla (Thai fish sauce)
soy kaffir butter sauce (see left)

1 Put the live lobsters on a small tray in the freezer for 2 hours. Remove the lobsters from the freezer and put straight into a large pot of boiling water. Return the water to a boil and cook for 4 minutes, then remove the lobsters from the water and cool. (This preparation can be done in advance.)

2 Preheat the broiler for 10–15 minutes at its highest setting. Lay each lobster belly-side down on a cutting board. Cut in half lengthwise, from head to tail, to give 4 halves in total.

3 Remove and discard the stomach sac and any intestinal tract that runs down the tail section alongside the shell.

4 Place the lobster halves, meat-side up, on a large baking tray. Season lightly, then brush liberally all over with the melted butter.

5 Place under the broiler and cook for 6–8 minutes until cooked through.

6 While the lobster is broiling, put the nam pla and soy kaffir butter sauce in a pan and bring to a boil.

7 Transfer the cooked lobster halves to 4 individual plates, spoon the sauce over them, and serve.

PG tip It is not just the cost that can put people off cooking lobsters, but the killing of them, too. This method with the freezer is the most humane way to do it: the lobsters simply fall asleep and die painlessly.

INDONESIAN GUACAMOLE

If you enjoy the famous Mexican guacamole, you'll love this Easternised variation, overlaid with the delicate flavors of Indonesia. ⊕ *Use as a spread to go in smoked salmon or roast chicken sandwiches.*

makes 1¼ cups

2 ripe (but not soft) Hass avocados

1 large vine tomato, cut into small pieces

1 tablespoon sambal oelek (see page 148)

10 Thai sweet basil leaves, torn into small pieces

1 red onion, finely chopped

juice of 3 limes

salt and freshly cracked black pepper

1 Cut the avocados in half and remove the pits. Using a spoon, scoop out the flesh into a bowl, then mash with a fork.

2 Add the remaining ingredients, with salt and pepper to taste. If you are not serving immediately, return the pits to the bowl to prevent the guacamole from going brown.

CHINESE TAHINI SAUCE

I love this sesame-flavored sauce and often serve it as part of a buffet salad, tossed with Chinese egg noodles. The tahini adds a richer flavor than using sesame oil alone. ⊕ *Toss noodles with the sauce at the last minute or use as a dipping sauce.*

makes ⅔ cup

2 tablespoons rice wine vinegar

½ teaspoon sugar

3½ tablespoons soy sauce

2 tablespoons sesame oil

¼ teaspoon dried red pepper flakes

1 tablespoon peanut oil

1 tablespoon tahini (sesame seed paste)

2 garlic cloves, crushed

1-inch piece of fresh ginger, peeled and
    finely chopped

4 scallions, finely chopped

1 Heat the vinegar and sugar in a small pan until the sugar has dissolved, transfer to a bowl, and whisk in the remaining ingredients. The sauce will keep in a sealed container in the fridge for several weeks.

LIME PICKLE VINAIGRETTE

There is something about lime pickle that I can't resist. I tend to eat most of it before the meal even begins, precariously piled onto spicy poppadoms, much to the annoyance of my fellow guests who never got a chance! ⊕ *Here is a play on an Indian-French vinaigrette idea; excellent served with grilled fish or grilled chicken, or poured over hot, steaming new potatoes.*

makes ⅔ cup

1 tablespoon chopped lime pickle
1 tablespoon chopped mint
½ tablespoon chopped cilantro leaves
¼ cup olive oil
juice of 2 limes
2 tablespoons classic vinaigrette (see page 62)
1 teaspoon nam pla (Thai fish sauce)
salt and freshly cracked black pepper

1 Put the lime pickle in a blender with the herbs and olive oil and blitz to a coarse puree.
2 Transfer to a bowl and add the remaining ingredients, with salt and pepper to taste.

ARUGULA AND YUZU CHUTNEY

Here I add a twist to a traditional Asian-style mint chutney, by substituting arugula for some of the mint. If you can't find yuzu (see page 170), fresh limes will do. ⊕ *This chutney is great for drizzling over rice dishes.*

makes ⅔ cup

a small handful of mint leaves
a small handful of arugula leaves
1 onion, chopped
juice of 2 yuzu (or limes), or ¼ cup bottled
    yuzu juice
2 tablespoons water
½ teaspoon garam masala

1 Put all the ingredients in a blender and blitz to a coarse puree, adding a little more water if necessary. Refrigerate in a sealed container for up to 2 days.

SWEET sauces

A sweet sauce can transform the plainest dessert into a culinary masterpiece, whether it's hot chocolate sauce poured over a poached pear, a simple fruit coulis to accompany vanilla ice cream, or a sweet flavored butter to melt over grilled figs or crêpes. A good range of dessert sauces will enrich your repertoire immeasurably, and they are not at all difficult or time-consuming to make. In this chapter you will find recipes for traditional favorites, such as a vanilla-laced crème anglaise or a richly indulgent toffee sauce, alongside lesser-known treasures, like Mexico's cajeta—a thick caramel sauce made with goat's milk. Simple flavored syrups can be prepared for keeping in stock, and used, when needed to add a special touch to many sweet dishes.

CRÈME ANGLAISE

Perhaps the greatest and best-loved of all dessert sauces. This is basically a creamy vanilla sauce, or custard, delicately flavored with a vanilla bean; it is also the basis for delicious vanilla ice cream.

makes about 3¼ cups

1¼ cups whole milk

scant cup whipping cream

1 vanilla bean, split lengthwise

6 cage-free egg yolks

⅔ cup sugar

1 Put the milk, cream, and vanilla bean in a heavy pan. Bring to a boil, then immediately remove from the heat and set aside to infuse for 15 minutes.
2 Meanwhile, using a beater, beat the egg yolks and sugar in a bowl until thick and creamy.
3 Pour the warm milk and cream mixture onto the egg mixture, beating continuously.
4 Return the mixture to the saucepan and cook over a low heat, stirring constantly with a wooden spoon until the custard thickens and coats the back of the spoon.
5 Remove from the heat, strain through a fine strainer, and either serve hot or let cool.

Variations

BRANDY SAUCE

Add 2 tablespoons brandy to the finished sauce. This also works well with Calvados, rum, or Poire William (pear eau de vie). Brandy sauce is traditionally served with British Christmas pudding (plum pudding), but the variations are great with pies and fruit puddings.

ALMOND MILK ANGLAISE

Bring the milk and cream to a boil with 1½ cups ground almonds, omitting the vanilla, and leave it overnight to infuse. Strain and use the almond-infused milk and cream mixture as in the basic recipe.

CITRUS ANGLAISE

Replace the vanilla bean in the milk and cream infusion with 2 tablespoons grated and blanched zest of lemon or orange. You can also add 1–2 tablespoons lemon curd sauce (see page 214) to the finished custard.

HERB-INFUSED ANGLAISE

I love infusing custards with fresh herbs, such as mint, lemon verbena, lemon thyme...the list is only as limited as your imagination. Add to the milk and cream infusion instead of the vanilla, then strain before you pour it onto the eggs.

SPICE-INFUSED ANGLAISE

Replace the vanilla in the milk and cream infusion with 1 teaspoon either ground cloves or ground star anise, or a stick of cinnamon. Great with autumn fruits, such as pears and apples.

CHESTNUT ANGLAISE

Replace the sugar with 3½ tablespoons chestnut honey, then stir 2 tablespoons chestnut puree into the finished sauce. A festive favorite of mine that usually makes an appearance around Christmas!

MOUSSELINE ANGLAISE

For a lighter custard, fold a good ⅓ cup lightly whipped cream into the finished, cold sauce.

TEA OR COFFEE ANGLAISE

Replace the vanilla bean in the milk and cream infusion with 2 tablespoons good-quality loose-leaf tea, such as Earl Grey or jasmine. For a coffee sauce, add 3 tablespoons prepared espresso coffee or 2 tablespoons Camp coffee essence or other coffee-flavored syrup to the finished sauce.

PG tip Leaving the vanilla-infused milk overnight will allow the vanilla to permeate better, and will improve the flavor.

Crème anglaise variation

SAFFRON ANGLAISE

Replace the vanilla in the milk and cream infusion with a generous pinch of good-quality saffron, then proceed as for the basic recipe. I love this with chocolate tart or poached pears.

CRÈME PÂTISSIÈRE

This custard-style cream is one of the basics of the pastry kitchen, and is used in numerous desserts and as a filling for such delicacies as profiteroles, French pastries, and tarts. Once made, it can be stored in the fridge, covered, for up to 2–3 days, but I find it is best to use it the same day. Even better than regular sugar here is vanilla sugar, if you have it.

makes 1½ cups

1¼ cups whole milk

⅓ cup sugar or vanilla sugar

1 vanilla bean, split lengthwise

4 cage-free egg yolks

2 teaspoons flour

1½ tablespoons chilled unsalted butter, cut into small pieces

1 Put the milk with half the sugar and the vanilla bean in a pan and bring to a boil. Remove from the heat immediately, then let infuse for 15 minutes.

2 In a bowl, beat the egg yolks with the remaining sugar until thick and light. Beat in the flour well.

3 Remove the vanilla bean from the milk and pour the milk into the egg mixture, beating constantly.

4 Return the mixture to the pan and bring it slowly to a boil over a low heat. Cook for 1–2 minutes, to allow the flour to cook.

5 Remove from the heat and whisk in the butter pieces. Let cool before using.

Variations

CHOCOLATE CRÈME PÂTISSIÈRE

Before you add the butter, stir 3½ ounces (about 1⅓ cups) grated good-quality dark chocolate (60–70 percent cocoa solids) into the warm sauce, until melted and smooth.

COFFEE CRÈME PÂTISSIÈRE

Add 2 tablespoons Camp coffee essence to the finished sauce before cooling.

ALMOND CRÈME PÂTISSIÈRE

Replace the milk in the basic recipe with almond milk.

ALCOHOL-INFUSED CRÈME PÂTISSIÈRE

Add 1 tablespoon of your preferred liquor to the finished sauce—for example rum, Cointreau, kirsch, or Poire William (eau de vie).

CHIBOUST SAUCE

Also known as crème Saint-Honoré, this is a lightened variation of crème pâtissière, used to fill profiteroles or to line the bottom of a fruit tart. Replace the flour with cornstarch and fold in 2 beaten egg whites to the finished, cooled sauce.

PG tip One of the most common mistakes in making this cream is to undercook it. You absolutely must cook it for a minute or two after it has boiled; you will notice a dramatic change in consistency as it becomes shinier, smoother, and thinner, rather than thick and pasty.

ZABAGLIONE

An Italian sauce, also often referred to by its French name, *sabayon*. Both are generally made with whipped eggs and Marsala wine, although other types of alcohol are often used instead of Marsala.

Many traditional zabaglione recipes do not include the whipped cream at the end, but I find it gives the sauce a better finish. ⊕ *It can be served warm, cold, or frozen, and is excellent with both fresh and poached fruit.*

makes 1¼ cups

6 cage-free egg yolks

⅓ cup sugar

¼ cup Marsala wine

scant ½ cup whipping cream, semi-whipped to soft peaks

1 Put the egg yolks, sugar, and Marsala in the top of a double boiler. Set the pan over simmering water, with the bottom of the pan just above the water.

2 Beat until the mixture becomes light and frothy, and doubled in volume.

3 Remove from the heat, then gradually add the semi-whipped cream, beating all the time until amalgamated.

4 Serve immediately or pour into glasses and let it go cold; either is delicious.

Variations

ORANGE SAUTERNES ZABAGLIONE

Add the grated and blanched zest of 1 orange to the egg yolks and replace the Marsala with sweet Sauternes. Wonderful with hot chocolate desserts.

HONEY ZABAGLIONE

Replace the sugar with 3 tablespoons honey, and the Marsala with Vin Santo.

ORANGE AND BASIL ZABAGLIONE

Add the grated and blanched zest of 1 orange to the egg yolks and replace the Marsala with orange liqueur. Finish the zabaglione with 1 tablespoon finely chopped basil—wonderful with oven-baked oranges.

CHOCOLATE ANISE ZABAGLIONE

Replace the Marsala with Ricard or Pernod. Fold ¼ cup melted white chocolate into the finished zabaglione. Superb with nectarines or chocolate mousse.

CHAMBORD ZABAGLIONE

Replace the Marsala with ¼ cup Chambord (raspberry) liqueur. My favorite way to serve this is to sprinkle some finely chopped preserved ginger on a dish of raspberries, then pour the Chambord sauce over them.

PG tip The Marsala can also be replaced by port, Calvados or one of my particular favorites, Bailey's Irish Cream, which makes a wicked sauce to serve with warm pear tart.

CREAMED CARAMEL SAUCE

Making your own caramel sauce can seem a bit of a daunting task to many people, but it doesn't have to be that way! Make sure you have the pans and ingredients ready and at hand before you start, and follow the basic steps carefully. It takes practically no time at all and is delicious for all sorts of desserts.

One note of caution: be extremely careful when cooking the sugar to caramel. Once heated, it will be considerably hotter than boiling water.

makes about 2 cups

3½ tablespoons liquid glucose

1 cup sugar

1¼ cups heavy cream

1¾ tablespoons unsalted butter, cut into
    small pieces

1 Put the liquid glucose in a deep, heavy pan and warm it over a low heat, without letting it boil. (It is important to use a deep pan, as the mixture foams up.)

2 Add the sugar, increase the heat, and simmer until caramelized to a rich, golden-amber color, about 2–3 minutes; the more caramelized the sugar, the more intense the flavor.

3 Shake the pan to distribute the color evenly, but do not stir. Use a wet pastry brush to brush any crystallizing sugar from the sides of the pan.

4 Meanwhile, bring the cream to a boil in a separate pan, remove from the heat, then pour the warm cream into the hot caramel, taking care as it will splatter.

5 Add the butter pieces and whisk the sauce until smooth. Remove from the heat and let cool before serving.

Variations

SALT CARAMEL SAUCE

Replace the unsalted butter with 3 tablespoons salted butter, plus an extra pinch of sea salt or kosher salt. Lovely served over ice cream or with a pear tart!

LIQUEUR CARAMEL SAUCE

Add 3½ tablespoons of your favorite liqueur to the finished sauce.

VANILLA CARAMEL SAUCE

Add 1 split vanilla bean to the cream before bringing it to a boil, then proceed as for the basic recipe and strain before using.

ORANGE CARAMEL SAUCE

Add the finely grated zest of 1 orange to the sugar and caramelize as for the basic recipe. Let cool before adding 2 tablespoons orange-flavored liqueur, such as Grand Marnier or Curaçao.

Clear caramel syrup
variation

POMEGRANATE CARAMEL SYRUP

Bring the basic clear
caramel syrup to a boil
with 1 tablespoon
pomegranate molasses.
Let cool before adding
¼ cup grenadine syrup.
Try it in the semifreddo
recipe opposite.

CLEAR CARAMEL SYRUP

Whenever I make this clear syrup it reminds me of my time training in a pastry department. Back then, caramel was traditionally made in copper-bottomed pans to retain a better overall heat. Now a heavy-bottomed pan gives a good result.

makes 1 cup

1 cup sugar

3½ tablespoons liquid glucose

6–7 tablespoons hot water

1 Put the sugar, liquid glucose, and half the cold water in a heavy pan and stir over a gentle heat with a wooden spoon until the sugar has dissolved.

2 Increase the heat and, as soon as the syrup reaches a boil, stop stirring and let it cook until dark caramel in color.

3 Remove from the heat, let cool slightly, then thin with the hot water.

Variations

VANILLA CARAMEL SYRUP

Split a vanilla bean lengthwise and scrape the seeds out into the pan of finished caramel. Add ¼ cup hot water, boil for 1 minute, then remove from the heat and let cool. Lovely with fruit tarts.

JASMINE CARAMEL SYRUP

Bring a scant ½ cup water to a boil, add 1 tablespoon jasmine tea leaves, and remove from the heat. Let infuse for 1 minute, then strain, reserving just the liquid. Add the infused tea liquid to the finished caramel syrup, simmer for 2 minutes, then let cool.

COFFEE CARAMEL SYRUP

Add 1 tablespoon Camp coffee essence to the finished clear caramel syrup. Wonderful poured over poached pears or bananas.

ICED WALNUT SEMIFREDDO WITH POMEGRANATE SYRUP AND PISTACHIOS

serves 4

½ cup caster sugar

¾ cup walnut halves

2 cage-free eggs

2½ ounces white chocolate, melted

1¼ cups heavy cream, semi-whipped to soft peaks

1 quantity pomegranate caramel syrup (see opposite)

2 tablespoons roughly chopped shelled pistachios

1 Put two thirds of the sugar in a heavy pan over a low heat. Gently melt the sugar, then increase the heat until it cooks to a dark caramel-amber color.

2 Add the walnuts and cook for 30 seconds. Pour the mixture out into a tray and let cool, then finely chop it into small pieces.

3 Put the eggs and remaining sugar in the top of a double boiler and place over simmering water. Beat until the mixture doubles in volume and becomes thick, dense, and creamy. Remove the pan from the heat and beat it again until cool.

4 Add the melted chocolate, then fold in the semi-whipped cream and the caramelized sugared nuts.

5 Pour into a plastic wrap-lined terrine or individual molds and place in the freezer overnight.

6 Remove the frozen semifreddo from the terrine or molds. Cut the terrine into slices or, if using individual molds, leave them whole. Pour the pomegranate syrup over them, sprinkle with the pistachios, and serve.

CAJETA SAUCE

I had to find a place in this book for this famous Mexican caramel sauce. It is traditionally made from fresh goat's or sheep's milk, cooked down very slowly until it becomes a luscious, enriched, caramelized cream. In Mexico it is sold in jars, but sadly I have found it hard to come by here, not for want of trying. Luckily, it's easy to recreate at home. ⊕ *Cajeta is traditionally served over ice cream or drizzled over pancakes or crêpes, but I love it with roasted bananas, or even pumpkin pie served for Thanksgiving. I also spread it thickly over bread or brioche, a real treat. Make plenty—it doesn't stick around for long!*

makes 3–3½ cups

3¼ cups goat's (or sheep's) milk

⅓ cup sugar

1 cup whipping cream

1 fat stick of cinnamon

3½ tablespoons chilled unsalted butter, cut into small pieces

1 Put the milk, sugar, cream, and cinnamon stick in a wide, heavy pan and bring to a boil.

2 Remove the cinnamon, lower the heat, and simmer gently for about 2 hours. It will go though varying color changes in this time, from light to dark caramel.

3 Remove from the heat and whisk in the butter. Serve warm or let it cool. The sauce will keep in a sealed jar in the fridge for 2 weeks.

VANILLA PANCAKES WITH ROASTED BANANAS AND CAJETA

serves 4

1 cup plus 2 tablespoons plain flour

1 tablespoon sugar

4 cage-free eggs

1 vanilla bean or 1 teaspoon vanilla extract

⅔ cup whipping cream

⅔ cup whole milk

vegetable oil, for frying

1¾ tablespoons unsalted butter

4 bananas, peeled and cut in half lengthwise

2 tablespoons confectioners' sugar

½ cup cajeta sauce (see left)

plain yogurt, for serving (optional)

1 Sift the flour into a bowl, stir in the sugar and eggs, and mix well.

2 Split the vanilla bean lengthwise and scrape out the seeds. Add the seeds, cream, and milk to the bowl and mix well to form a smooth batter. Let it rest for 1 hour.

3 Heat a little oil in a large nonstick frying pan. Using a 2-inch-wide ladle, spoon some of the batter in heaps around the pan, far enough apart to ensure they will not touch each other as they spread.

4 Cook until just golden around the edges—about 1 minute—then flip each pancake over and cook on the other side for another minute, until golden. Remove from the pan and keep warm. Repeat until all the batter is used up, making 8 small pancakes in total.

5 Meanwhile, heat the butter in another frying pan and add the bananas. Dust with confectioners' sugar and cook until golden and caramelized.

6 Place 2 banana halves between 2 pancakes on each serving plate. Pour a little cajeta over them and top with a spoonful of yogurt, if using.

BUTTERSCOTCH SAUCE

The Scotch is optional but traditional here. Adding golden syrup to the basic toffee sauce undoubtedly results in a more malty flavor.

makes 2½ cups

⅓ cup soft brown sugar
⅔ cup heavy cream
3½ tablespoons unsalted butter
½ cup golden syrup
½ teaspoon vanilla extract
1 tablespoon Scotch whisky (optional)

1 Put the sugar, cream, butter, and syrup in a heavy pan and cook gently over a low heat, stirring with a wooden spoon until the butter has melted and the sugar has dissolved.
2 Increase the heat and bring to a boil, stirring constantly. Lower the heat again and simmer for 8–10 minutes until the color changes from a milky coffee to a rich caramel.
3 Remove from the heat, stir in the vanilla extract, and whisky if using, and serve warm.

Variations

As with many sweet sauces, a dash of your favorite tipple (rum, brandy, or Grand Marnier, for example) will always work. Or choose from the variations listed below.

CRÈME FRAÎCHE
BUTTERSCOTCH SAUCE
Add 2 tablespoons crème fraîche to the finished sauce to add a little tanginess.

COCONUT BUTTERSCOTCH SAUCE
Replace half the cream with thick coconut milk and use 2½ tablespoons rather than ½ cup golden syrup.

GINGER BUTTERSCOTCH SAUCE
Add ½ teaspoon ground ginger to the ingredients at the start of the basic recipe.

TOFFEE SAUCE

This sauce and the butterscotch one on the left are often interchangeable, and indeed are basically one and the same. My research leads me to believe that toffee sauce originated in Britain and the Scots added golden syrup to create butterscotch sauce. Both are simple to make, rich and very addictive.
⊕ *Either sauce is wonderful poured over ice cream or served with steamed sponge puddings.*

makes 1¾ cups

1 cup soft brown sugar
scant ½ cup heavy cream
1 stick minus 1 tablespoon unsalted butter
½ teaspoon vanilla extract

1 Make in the same way as butterscotch sauce (see left), but simmer for only 4–5 minutes so that the sauce does not turn as dark.

PG tip Both sauces can be prepared in advance and kept in an airtight container in the fridge for up to 10 days. Return either sauce to room temperature before serving.

CHOCOLATE SAUCE

If you start with good-quality chocolate, making a great-tasting chocolate sauce is a simple task. Different cooks prefer different chocolates but they all agree that it's vital to use one with at least 60–70 percent cocoa solids. This is the one thing to get right; after that, some cooks use water, some milk, some cream. All work well in their own way, and create sauces of different qualities.

makes 1¾ cups

1 cup light or heavy cream

2 tablespoons sugar

4 ounces dark chocolate (60–70 percent cocoa solids), broken into small pieces

1¾ tablespoons unsalted butter

1 Put the cream and sugar in a heavy pan and bring slowly to a boil.

2 Immediately remove from the heat and stir in the chocolate and butter until melted and smooth.

3 Serve warm or let cool.

Variations

BOOZY CHOCOLATE SAUCE

Add 2 tablespoons rum, Grand Marnier, or another preferred liquor to the finished sauce.

GINGER CHOCOLATE SAUCE

Infuse the cream and sugar with 1 teaspoon ground ginger, then proceed as for the basic recipe.

LAVENDER CHOCOLATE SAUCE

Infuse the cream and sugar with 1 teaspoon lavender leaves and proceed as for the basic recipe, but strain before cooling. This is also very good with the same quantity of rosemary or thyme leaves.

WHITE CHOCOLATE SAUCE

White chocolate, although not technically a chocolate at all, makes a good sauce alternative to the dark chocolate versions. My wife Anita is a bit of a white-chocolate-lover, so I often make this at home for her.

makes 1½ cups

7 ounces white chocolate, grated or broken into small pieces

1 cup heavy cream

¼ cup whole milk

2 teaspoons unsalted butter

1 tablespoon kirsch (optional)

1 Melt the chocolate in the top of a double boiler over simmering water.

2 Put the cream and milk in a separate pan and bring to a boil.

3 Pour the cream and milk mixture into the melted chocolate, then add the butter and stir with a wooden spoon until melted and smooth. Stir in the kirsch, if using, and serve warm or let cool before using.

Variation

Finish the chocolate sauce with 1 tablespoon anise liquor, such as Pernod or Ricard—delicious.

Fruit coulis variation

MANGO COULIS

Replace the red fruits with
2 ripe mangoes, peeled and
cut into chunks.

FRUIT COULIS

Coulis, made from pureed, strained fruit, is one of the simplest of all the dessert sauces to prepare. Fruit sauces add not only a fresh taste to desserts, but also a splash of color and fragrance. They are traditionally served cold, but can also be served hot.

Fresh or frozen fruits can be used for coulis, and how much sugar you add will depend on the variety of fruit used, as well as on its state of maturity; you will need to adjust the proportion of sugar to match these varying conditions. ⊕ *Wonderful served with fruit tarts, puddings, or simply poured over ice creams and sherbets—a winner every time.*

PG tip Take care not to over-blend the fruits, as I find it lightens the color and removes their natural freshness. For fruits with a tarter flavor, such as red currants, add double the amount of sugar, bring to a boil, and cool before blending.

RED BERRY COULIS

You can use just a single type of berry for this sauce, or make up a mixture of soft summer fruits, as I have here.

makes 2½ cups
8 ounces raspberries (about 1¾–2 cups)
8 ounces strawberries, hulled
2 tablespoons confectioners' sugar
1 tablespoon water
a few drops of lemon juice, to taste

1 Put the fruits in a blender with the confectioners' sugar and the water. Blitz for 20 seconds until smooth, then add the lemon juice.
2 Adjust the sweetness with more sugar if necessary, then strain through a strainer and serve.

Variation
NECTARINE AND PEACH COULIS
Replace the red fruits with 4 ripe nectarines or peaches. Remove the pits, cut the flesh into pieces, and proceed as for the basic recipe.

BAKED LEMON PUDDING
WITH RED BERRY COULIS

In this dessert the lemon juice provides not only the base for a wonderful light pudding but also a tangy lemon sauce, beneath it. The red berry coulis acts as the perfect balance for the tart lemon flavor.

serves 4

1 tablespoon flour

1 cup plus 2 tablespoons sugar

grated zest of ½ lemon, preferably unwaxed

¼ cup lemon juice

4 cage-free eggs, separated

1 cup whole milk

a pinch of salt

scant cup red berry coulis (see page 211),
   for serving

1 Preheat the oven to 350°F. Sift the flour into a bowl, then add the sugar and the lemon zest and juice.

2 In a separate bowl, beat the egg yolks and milk together. Add to the flour and sugar mixture and stir well to mix.

3 In a clean bowl and using clean beaters, beat the egg whites with the salt until stiff, then, using a rubber spatula, carefully fold into the batter.

4 Pour into 4 lightly greased, shallow, ovenproof dishes. Place in a baking pan and pour boiling water into the pan until it reaches halfway up the dishes, to make a water bath.

5 Bake for 45 minutes until golden, light, and fluffy. Serve with the berry coulis on the side.

OTHER FRUIT SAUCES

The sauces that follow here are all standard recipes, and perfectly good for it. But that shouldn't stop you playing around with the basic recipes to add extra interest and complexity, by infusing them with flavors of your choice. Lemon verbena, for example, makes a wonderful addition to the lemon sauce.

JAM SAUCE

makes 1 cup

½ cup good-quality jam (such as raspberry, strawberry, fig)

1 teaspoon arrowroot, mixed with 2 teaspoons water

1 Put the jam in a heavy pan with 5 tablespoons water and bring to a boil. Stir in the dissolved arrowroot, and cook for 1 minute.

2 Remove any scum from the surface of the sauce and strain through a fine strainer.

LEMON SAUCE

makes 1½ cups

grated zest and juice of 2 lemons

⅓ cup caster sugar

2½ tablespoons arrowroot, mixed with 2 tablespoons water

1 Put the lemon zest and juice in a heavy pan along with 1¼ cups water and sugar and bring to a boil.

2 Whisk in the dissolved arrowroot and cook for 30 seconds, then strain through a fine strainer.

PG tip Other citrus fruits, such as grapefruit, mandarins, oranges, and so on can be substituted for lemons, with the quantity of sugar adjusted to the sweetness of the fruit.

LEMON CURD SAUCE

makes 1 cup

1 cup plus 2 tablespoons sugar

½ cup (1 stick) unsalted butter

finely grated zest and juice of 3 large, unwaxed lemons

3 large cage-free eggs, beaten

1 Put the sugar, butter, and lemon zest and juice in a heavy pan.

2 Heat gently, stirring, until the sugar has dissolved and the butter has melted.

3 Add the eggs, stirring constantly over a low heat, until the curd thickens and leaves the sides of the pan clean. Remove from the heat and transfer to a jar. When cool, cover and refrigerate.

FLAVORED SYRUP SAUCES

Sugar-based syrups are an easy way to prepare a simple yet delicious sauce for desserts. They are wonderful poured over ice cream, or drizzled over seasonal fruit salads or delicate mousses. I include two recipes, one for basic syrup and one for a caramel syrup: both form the base of many great sauces.

BASIC SYRUP

makes 1 cup

scant ½ cup water
1 cup sugar
scant ½ cup liquid glucose

1 Put the water, sugar, and liquid glucose in a heavy pan and stir with a wooden spoon until the sugar has dissolved.
2 Heat the syrup and as soon as it reaches a boil, stop stirring and cook for 1 minute, until a lightly thickened syrup sauce forms.
3 Remove from the heat, transfer to a bowl, and let cool.

Variations

ORANGE BLOSSOM SYRUP

Put 1 quantity of basic syrup in a pan with the finely grated zest of 1 orange and the juice of 4 oranges. Boil for 2–3 minutes, let cool, then add 1 tablespoon orange blossom water.

GINGER AND LIME SYRUP

Put 1 quantity of basic syrup in a pan with 2 tablespoons preserved ginger syrup, the juice of 3 limes, and a finely chopped, peeled 1-inch piece of fresh ginger. Boil for 2–3 minutes, then let cool.

SOFT FRUIT SYRUP

Place a small colander over a bowl. Lay a double thickness of cheesecloth inside the colander, then add about 2 cups fresh or frozen soft fruit, such as raspberries, strawberries, or black currants. Bring 1 quantity of basic syrup to a boil in a small pan, then pour it over the fruits. Leave overnight in the fridge to let the fruits release their juices into the bowl, to give a clear syrup. Stir in 1 tablespoon of fruit liqueur such as kirsch.

LAVENDER SYRUP

Put 1 quantity of basic syrup and 1 teaspoon lavender leaves in a small pan and bring to a boil. Remove from the heat and let infuse for 30 minutes, then strain.

RED WINE SYRUP

Put ⅔ cup red wine (Syrah or cabernet sauvignon) in a pan with ½ stick of cinnamon, 1 clove, and ½ vanilla bean, and boil until reduced by half. Add 1 quantity of basic syrup and cook for 10 minutes, then strain and cool. Other wines and liquors such as champagne, rum, and port also make great syrup.

PG tip Always ensure the sugar has completely dissolved before bringing it to a boil, and remember not to stir once it has reached boiling point, however tempting that may be!

Basic syrup variation

HERB SYRUP

Blanch a good handful
(1¾ ounces) of the chopped
herb of your choice—mint,
basil, and cilantro are
ideal—in boiling water for
10 seconds, then quickly
remove to a bowl of ice
water. Drain, dry, then blitz
in a blender with the basic
syrup. Strain through a fine
mesh strainer or double
thickness of cheesecloth.

MOROCCAN BAKLAVA WITH ORANGE BLOSSOM SYRUP

This is my version of the famous Greek dessert, popular throughout the whole Mediterranean region. The Moroccan element comes in the fragrance and light spicing synonymous with the country's cuisine.

serves 4

3½ ounces fresh dates, stones removed, finely chopped
2 cups walnut halves
1⅓ cups whole almonds
⅓ cup granulated sugar
2 tablespoons orange blossom water
1 teaspoon ground cinnamon
¼ teaspoon ground cloves
scant ½ cup orange juice
18 sheets of phyllo pastry dough, 8 x 12 inches
5 tablespoons (¾ stick) unsalted butter, melted
orange blossom syrup (see page 215), to taste

1 Put the dates, walnuts, and almonds in a blender and blitz to a paste.

2 Transfer to a bowl, add the sugar, orange blossom water, cinnamon, cloves, and half of the orange juice and mix well. Preheat the oven to 325°F.

3 Place a sheet of phyllo pastry dough in a 8 x 12-inch baking pan and brush with the melted butter. Top with 6 more sheets of phyllo, brushing each sheet well with melted butter.

4 Spread half the nut filling evenly over the surface, then top with 6 more sheets of phyllo, brushing each sheet with butter before adding the next.

5 Top with the remaining filling and the remaining phyllo sheets, brushing each sheet with butter in the same way.

6 Cut the baklava into diamond shapes in the pan and bake for 20–25 minutes, until an even golden color all over. Remove from the oven and let stand for 5 minutes. Pour some orange blossom syrup over the top and serve.

SWEET COMPOUND BUTTERS

These sweet compound butters make a simple, very flexible sauce or topping for all sorts of hot desserts, such as steamed puddings or crumbles. They are also delicious on warm toasted sweet buns, pancakes, waffles, or simply toast. All the recipes below use ½ cup (1 stick) softened, unsalted butter and follow the method outlined in the savory butter recipes on page 36.

LAVENDER HONEY BUTTER

Add 2 tablespoons lavender honey and ¼ teaspoon lavender leaves to the butter, then beat until smooth. Proceed as for the savory butter, rolling it up in plastic wrap. Especially good with figs.

RUM AND RAISIN BUTTER

Add 1–2 drops of vanilla extract, 2 tablespoons soft brown sugar, ¼ cup rum, and 2 tablespoons soaked raisins to the butter, then beat until smooth. Proceed as for the savory butter, rolling it up in plastic wrap.

CINNAMON BUTTER

Add 3 tablespoons confectioners' sugar and 1 tablespoon ground cinnamon to the butter, then beat until smooth. Proceed as for the savory butter, rolling it up in plastic wrap.

CHOCOLATE BUTTER

Add 4½ ounces finely grated, dark chocolate, 2 tablespoons confectioners' sugar, and 2 tablespoons crème de cacao liqueur to the butter, then beat until smooth. Proceed as for the savory butter, rolling it up in plastic wrap.

COFFEE BUTTER

Add ¼ cup confectioners' sugar and 2 tablespoons Camp coffee essence to the butter and beat until smooth. Proceed as for the savory butter, rolling it up in plastic wrap.

GRILLED FIGS EN BRIOCHE WITH LAVENDER BUTTER AND GOAT CHEESE

I make these when I'm in the mood for something a little different for Sunday brunch.

serves 4

5½ ounces soft goat cheese
1 tablespoon honey, heated
4 firm, ripe figs
½ cup sugar
4 slices of good-quality brioche
3½ tablespoons lavender honey butter (see left)

1 Preheat the broiler to its highest setting. Put the goat cheese and warmed honey in a bowl and stir with a wooden spoon to mix and soften.

2 Cut the figs in half and sprinkle the cut sides with the sugar. Place under the hot broiler until caramelized. (Alternatively, do this with a blow torch.)

3 Toast the brioche slices until golden and top each with 2 slices of lavender butter, then return to the broiler to melt gently.

4 Place 2 fig halves on each brioche slice, with a good spoonful of the goat cheese on the side, and serve.

WEIGHT (solids)

½ oz.	15g
1 oz.	30g
1½ oz.	40g
2 oz.	55g
2½ oz.	70g
3 oz.	85g
3½ oz.	100g
4 oz.	115g
5 oz.	140g
6 oz.	170g
7 oz.	200g
8 oz. (½ lb.)	225g
9 oz.	255g
10 oz.	285g
11 oz.	310g
12 oz.(¾ lb.)	340g
14 oz.	400g
15 oz.	425g
1 lb.	450g
1 lb. 2oz.	500g
1¼ lb.	570g
1½ lb.	680g
1¾ lb.	790g
2lb	900g
2¼lb	1kg
3 lb.	1.4kg
4 lb.	1.8kg
4½ lb.	2kg
5 lb.	2.25kg
6½ lb.	3kg

VOLUME (liquids)

5 ml	1 teaspoon
15ml	1 tablespoon (½ fl. oz.)
30ml	2 tablespoons (1 fl. oz.)
60ml	¼ cup (2 fl. oz.)
90ml	6 tablespoons (3 fl. oz.)
120ml	½ cup (4 fl. oz.)
150ml	about ⅔ cup (5 fl. oz.)
180ml	¾ cup (6 fl. oz.)
200ml	7 fl. oz.
240ml	1 cup (8 fl. oz.)
300ml	1¼ cups (10 fl. oz.)
350ml	1½ cups (12 fl. oz.)
400ml	1¾ cups (14 fl. oz.)
480ml	1 pint (16 fl. oz.)
500ml (½ liter)	17 fl. oz.
540ml	2¼ cups (18 fl. oz.)
600ml	2½ cups (20 fl. oz.)
650ml	2¾ cups (22 fl. oz.)
700ml	3 cups (24 fl. oz.)
950ml	(1 quart) (32 fl. oz.)
1 liter	33.8 fl. oz.
1.2 liters	5 cups (40 fl. oz.)
1.4 liters	1½ quarts (48 fl. oz.)
1.9 liters	½ gallon (64 fl. oz.)
2 liters	8½ cups (68 fl. oz.)
3.8 liters	1 gallon (128 fl. oz.)

LENGTH

6mm	¼ in
1.3cm	½ in
1.9cm	¾ in
2.5cm	1 in
5cm	2 in
7.5cm	3 in
10cm	4 in
12.5cm	5 in
15cm	6 in
18cm	7 in
20.5cm	8 in
23cm	9 in
25.5cm	10 in
28cm	11 in
30.5cm	12 in (1 foot)